# SYMBOLS OF SALVATION

# SYMBOLS
## OF
# SALVATION

## DON M. AYCOCK

**BROADMAN PRESS**
Nashville, Tennessee

Library of Congress Catalog Card Number: 81-70976
Dewey Decimal Classification: 232.954
Subject heading: JESUS CHRIST—TEACHINGS

Printed in the United States of America

# Acknowledgments

No book is ever written in a vacuum. Even the author who wants to "get away from it all" and moves into a chalet in the backwoods of Vermont knows fully well that he or she owes much to countless people. I fully confess that I likewise owe much to many people who have helped me along life's pilgrimage, and whose fingerprints are all over this book.

First, I dedicate this work to my twin boys, Ryan and Christopher, who are four months old at this writing. They have given me an extra shot of adrenalin, and have made life "interesting."

Next, my wife Carla has been her usual supportive self through the entire painful process of putting these ideas on paper.

Barry Dennis, a pastor friend in Elizabethtown, Kentucky, has patiently given his ear to me while I expounded some of the ideas in this book (and then he would smile and ask for a second cup of coffee).

Herb Morgan, a funeral director in Louisville, taught me by his actions the symbolic role of caring for the bereaved.

The wonderful folks at West Side-Portland Baptist Church in Louisville patiently sat through worship services as the pastor "tried out" some of these ideas in the form of sermons.

Beverly Scherzinger and Laura Settle probably lost 30 percent of their vision trying to transcribe my original manuscript into readable copy.

Tom O'Neal, director of pastoral care at Highland Baptist Hospital in Louisville, motivated me indirectly by asking, "You mean you're writing *another* book?" Thanks Tom, I needed that!

And finally, I thank the staff of Broadman Press for serving as a catalyst for my writing.

I love these folks. They have taught me to live, to love, and to invest myself in the lives of others. My hope is that everyone could have friends like these.

# Preface

When I was a student at Louisiana College, I wanted for a while to major in philosophy. The depth of thought and the sheer abstractness of those ideas captivated me. I loved toying with terms such as "being" and "ontology" and "cosmology," among others. I thought then that, once I put all of these high-sounding terms and ideas under my belt, I would become an effective preacher and minister. After all, hadn't everyone heard of Paul Tillich and Alfred North Whitehead?

My "conversion" from that point of view came unexpectedly for me—I read the Bible! I began to see in the New Testament that Jesus did not speak in lofty, abstract terms. His recorded words are full of life and movement. He "peopled" his messages and captured his hearers with the ordinary. Jesus used the everyday things, events, and people of his time to communicate the depth of his faith and knowledge.

Jesus' symbolic use of common things in life made me rethink the whole business of communication. The substance of this book consists in my attempt to look with freshness at Jesus' methods of communicating truth. He did so by pointing to a deeper reality in the things which people saw daily.

Jesus took a coin and helped people reexamine their priorities. He took a child and made people want to be a child of and for God. He took a towel and impressed on his disciples the need for humble service. He took a cross and acted out his words, "I love you."

Jesus used these things, and others, symbolically. The word "symbol" comes from two Greek words, *syn*, meaning "together," and *ballein*, meaning "to throw." A symbol is "a sign, mark, or token, implying the throwing together or joining of an abstract idea and a visible sign of it; the sign serving to recall it, not by remembrance, but by suggestion."[1]

Most of us have difficulty finding the exact words to explain what Jesus means to the life and well-being of mankind. But the early church found that by using the cross as a symbol, for example, they could communicate that meaning without having to use many words. Of course, times have changed. Today many people use the cross as a piece of jewelry to be worn around the neck instead of as a communicator of God's love. The church today must explain its symbols to those who do not understand them.

Bruce Lockerbie raises some important questions we Christians must think about. He asks, "Is there some mystical quality . . . inherent in the signs and symbols familiar to Christians? If so, then what transforms a cross, burning on the lawn of a black family, into a symbol of hatred? When is a fish a visual acronym for *Jesus Christ, God's Son, Savior,* and when is it a logotype for a seafood restaurant? When is a bird a sign of the dove, and not merely a pigeon?"[2]

Symbols are also useful to people in the church for supplementing the teaching of doctrine and matters of faith. Damasus Winzen wrote, "Through his symbols, the Risen Saviour, exercises continuously his healing, integrating, illuminating power in the faithful. The symbols of Christ are more than clever means to convey an idea through external signs; they are a means to share in the life of the Saviour in such a way that the whole being of man is involved."[3]

"Salvation" is a word we throw around so much that we sometimes forget what it means. Basically it means wholeness, well-being, and togetherness. It refers to these qualities in our relationship to God, to others, to ourselves, and to our world. I like Frank Stagg's definition: "Salvation is not the reduction of life through asceticism or otherwise. It does not mean the rejection of the body. Neither does it mean the surrender of the intelligence or freedom of will. Jesus came to give life in abundance (John 10:10), not to shrink it. Salvation is not becoming an ascetic fragment through rejection of the body, nor is it becoming an angel or a ghost. It is to become a human being, nothing more and nothing less. It is to come into such relationship with God that one is freed from all such destructive forces as greed, lust, envy, jealousy, fear, prejudice, and hate. It is to be cleansed and renewed. It is to be given new direction and new resources for life. It is to come alive! It is to become a true human being in all the aspects of a unitary or holistic existence."[4]

Salvation is truly coming alive. This is why the term "new birth" is such an apt description. So this book is about the ways Jesus communicated such an existence. It is about the *Symbols of Salvation*.

# Contents

# Contents

# 1
# He Took a Child

*Mark 9:33-36*

Many moderns have great difficulty believing in a God who would have anything to do with them. Many seem to feel that if God exists at all (a proposition which is not self-evident), his existence is detached and illusive. The Deists once suggested that God made the world just as a watchmaker builds a watch. God wound up the world, sent it off spinning into space to wind down on its own. He had nothing else to do with his world. This view of God is held by many people today, although they may not use Deism for their belief. To them God is something of an "absentee landlord."

This idea comes to us from at least two sources. The first is ancient Greek philosophy. The Greeks thought of God as being like a rock in the sense that he never changes. The implication was that if God never changes, then he could not be actively involved in the daily affairs of the world. The second source of this idea is the day-to-day experience of many people. With all manner of evil and pain surrounding and affecting them, many persons simply see no signs of a compassionate spiritual Being who keeps his hands on the steering wheel of the world's machine.

Standing over against this Deistic view of God is the belief that God does exist in a manner which makes him known to people. He shows himself to be a loving, caring Being who is eminently interested in the affairs of this world. Classic Christian faith teaches that God has made himself known to mankind in the person

13

of Jesus of Nazareth. Jesus spent about the last three years of his life trying to show people what God was like and what he demanded from them. Jesus utilized various methods for doing this. He told parables and stories. He directly confronted people with the errors of their thought and action. And he used the common events, objects, and people around him as symbols of his message. This book will look at some of those symbols to find out who God is and how we are related to him. These events, objects, and people are *symbols of salvation.*

Salvation in the New Testament is a many-sided word which basically means a proper relationship to God. It points to wholeness and security of the believer and conveys the sense of belonging to God. Jesus used many different symbols to paint pictures of this salvation. One of those symbols was the children who were often around him.

Adults flocked to hear Jesus. They came for many reasons— curiosity, entertainment, and even disdain. Baby sitters probably were not heard of, so the children accompanied their parents. Can't you imagine the chaos surrounding Jesus and his disciples? People pushed and cursed, dogs barked, and children got underfoot. We are told that the disciples tried to keep the children away from Jesus so he could get on with more "important" things. But he rejected religion stamped "For Adults Only." I know some parents who have this idea. "We aren't going to push Jane into making any religious choices. We'll let her make her own choice about religion when she gets older. We wouldn't want to warp the child." Of course, they feel free to decide all other important matters for Jane including education, life-style, homelife, and the like.

Jesus seemed to think little of the disciples' efforts to block the children from being around him. As the biblical writer put it, he became "indignant." In essence, Jesus said, "Don't stop them from coming to me. God loves all people, even little ones." Jesus put his arms around the children and blessed them.

*Jesus took a child.* When you think about it, perhaps it seems odd that the same God who created the Grand Canyon and Niagara Falls would have anything to do with a little, seemingly insignificant child. But then what is Christmas all about? Jesus tried to show that God is far more concerned with persons than with gorges or waterfalls. For all their natural beauty, these natural places are nothing at all compared with the creative potential of one little boy or girl.

An Italian film entitled "Tree of the Wooden Clogs" portrays the plight of Italian peasants at the close of the nineteenth century. In one scene the village priest is shown talking with the poor parents of a five-year-old boy. The boy's father wants him to stay at home, work around the farm, and help support the family. The priest tells him the family must send the boy to school since God has given the boy the gift of intelligence. He explains that the potential of the whole world is wrapped up in that fuzzy-headed boy. The parents agree, at first reluctantly, to send the boy to school. They know the priest is right. Jesus knew what the priest realized—children hold the world's potential in their often dirty little hands.

Jesus was not only interested in their potential, but also in their worth as human beings in their own right. We adults almost always ask kids what they intend to be when they grow up. Is it because we assume they are nothing now? I have to agree with a comment by Franklin P. Jones, "Children are unpredictable. You never know what inconsistency they're going to catch you in next." They don't have to grow up for that!

Jesus' words and attitudes make a forceful commentary on the effectiveness of Mary and Joseph as parents. As Jesus thought about his own childhood he reflected the love and devotion Mary and Joseph had given to him. His attitude was remarkable because children were often seen in Jesus' day as mere mouths to feed and objects of aggravation. But Jesus saw the worth of children, both to their families and to God. Eric Marshall and Stuart Hample have written a delightful book entitled *Children's Letters to God*. One letter is from a boy named Glenn. He wrote, "Dear God, It's very good the way each kid has one mother and one father. Did it take you long to think of that?" It probably did. At least it was no off-the-cuff decision.

Jesus saw children as keys to the kingdom of God. But why children of all people? Why not the Pharisees or the Sadducees? Let me suggest several reasons why I think Jesus took a child as his example for entering the kingdom.

*1. The first has to do with the effects children have on other people.* A group of adults can melt when someone comes into their presence with a child, especially an infant. Why is that? I think most of us "ooh" and "ahh" over children because we really would like to be more loving, kind, and generous. But we are often afraid others will think we are silly or will take advantage of us. We are supposed to be tough and self-sufficient (at least this is a misguided American myth). But if we are loving toward children, our society says it's OK. The taboo is lifted. Brett Harte wrote a famous story called "The Luck of Roaring Camp." The story is about a wild mining camp where roughness and crudeness were the order of the day. A pregnant woman in the camp gave birth to a boy and then died. The rough old miners were left to care for the infant. Significant changes began to occur around Roaring Camp. Whereas the place before had always been filthy, the camp, and especially the child's room, was kept immaculate. Swearing was strictly forbidden. The favorite pastime after work had been drinking, but after the child came most of the miners spent their evenings looking after "their" child.

Children naturally seem to have a positive influence on other people. This is not always the case. Sam Levenson once cracked, "Insanity is hereditary; you get it from your children." Even so, Jesus knew that children were good symbols of salvation.

A recent film, *Being There*, portrays Peter Sellers as a near

moron known as "Chance the Gardener." He grew up in the
employment of a wealthy patron and knew nothing about the world
outside of his employer's house, except for what he saw on
television. Chance was forced to seek room and board elsewhere
when his master died. Because of his total naivete people were
naturally drawn to him. Others saw Chance as a brilliant economist
when in reality he was incredibly ignorant. The point is that his
child-like qualities attracted others.

2. *Children are a symbol of salvation because of their openness.*
One of the New Testament words for salvation is "new birth." This
term suggests that salvation is a radical new beginning. We begin
the process as spiritual children. As with all children, the children
of the kingdom of God must ever be open to learning, growing, and
cooperation with others.

I will never forget walking down a hall at St. Anthony Hospital in
Louisville one afternoon. I followed a couple who had three-year-
old twin boys walking behind them. The father turned around and
said to the twins, "Now join hands so you won't get lost." They did,
then turned around and saw me following. One of the boys held up
his hand to me and said, "Join hands." The fact that they were
black and I was white made absolutely no difference to them or me.
I took his hand, and we strolled down the hall like old friends. The
father turned around. When he saw what had happened he began to
laugh aloud. It was contagious because I started to belly-laugh, and
then the twins joined in. I'm sure if someone had been watching
they would have thought all of us were crazy. But it did not matter
what anyone else thought. I saw the face of God in the faces of
those happy children, and I knew a little better what Jesus meant
when he taught, "To such belong the kingdom of God."

All children of God are to be open and permeable. A mother and
girl were riding a train one day. The little girl kept looking out the
window and saying things like, "Look mother, a horse. Oh, look,
houses." As this kept up for a while, the somewhat embarrassed

mother said to the person seated next to her, "I'm sorry she is going on like this. She still thinks everything is wonderful." That mother was a candidate for the "Dope-of-the-Day" award!

Jesus knew that his followers would be faced with new and strange situations and decisions. He noted that the movement of God among them was like the blowing wind. No one who is inflexible and unwilling to learn can be a Christian. Thus Jesus' example: "You must be like this child."

3. *Children, as well as being open and flexible, are willing to try to carry their own weight.* I well remember my childhood days in rural Louisiana. My parents bought a sixteen-acre homestead and turned it into a mini-farm. We had a large truck patch and raised cattle and ducks. I even had an alligator for a while. As I look back on those idyllic days, I'm sure I was often in the way. My father told me that it was easier for him to do most of the chores himself than to teach me and my brother how to do them. I can say to his credit and my benefit that he exercised patience and did teach us much. The point is that we wanted to learn and help.

I am convinced that Jesus wanted his followers to have that same child-like quality. Many Christians are like a donkey in one of Aesop's fables. This animal was loaded down with packs of salt. As he crossed a stream on a narrow bridge he lost his footing and slipped into the water. The salt dissolved, and the donkey had no burden to carry the rest of that day. The next day he crossed the same stream. Remembering what had happened on the previous day the donkey deliberately fell into the water. The trick did not work and his burden was even heavier. He had been loaded with sponges. Many of us have sought to evade our duties and slough off our responsibilities, but our Lord reminds us, in essence, "Look at a child. He will try anything and isn't afraid of failure." Roger Lewin underscored the problem when he observed, "Too often we give children answers to remember rather than problems to solve."

Yes, children do think all things are wonderful, and they are open to all of God's creation. They are not blinded by the cataracts of racial prejudice, nor are they chained by suspicion, hatred, and rebellion. Truly they are symbols of God's plan for all of his people.

Following Jesus' command to be like children is certainly no easy task. Our lives can become jungles, with our religious concerns choked out, rather than well-weeded gardens. Genesis speaks of Adam's fall, but in a real sense each of us experiences our own personal fall. As we grow older we lose those qualities of openness and wonder which characterize children. As psychologist Eric Berne observed, "The moment the little boy is concerned with which is a jay and which is a sparrow, he can no longer see the birds or hear them sing." Part of this is a natural and necessary process, but not all of it. Our tendencies to become rigid and cynical attest to the reality of sin in our lives. Recapturing Eden is never easy.

### WHAT I LIVE FOR

I live for those who love me,
　　Whose hearts are kind and true;
For the Heaven that smiles above me,
　　And awaits my spirit too;
For all human ties that bind me,
For the task by God assigned me,
For the bright hopes yet to find me,
　　And the good that I can do.

I live to learn their story
　　Who suffered for my sake;
To emulate their glory,
　　And follow in their wake;
Bards, patriots, martyrs, sages,
The heroic of all ages,
Whose deeds crowd History's pages,
　　And Time's great volume make.

I live to hold communion
　　With all that is divine,

To feel there is a union
   Twixt Nature's heart and mine;
To profit by affliction,
Reap truth from fields of fiction,
Grow wiser from conviction,
   And fulfil God's grand design.

I live to hail that season
   By gifted ones foretold,
When men shall live by reason,
   And not alone by gold;
When man to man united,
And every wrong thing righted,
The whole world shall be lighted
   As Eden was of old.

I live for those who love me,
   For those who know me true,
For the Heaven that smiles above me,
   And awaits my spirit too;
For the cause that lacks assistance,
For the wrong that needs resistance,
For the future in the distance,
   And the good that I can do.[2]

*4. Children are symbols of salvation because of their confidence.*
They are like bumblebees—they cannot fly, aerodynamically
speaking, but they do. Children do all kinds of things adults say
they cannot do. They do not know that you can't trust people, so
they do. They do not know that you can't love all people, regardless
of the color of their skin, so they do. And in doing so they put
adults to shame and teach us about God if we will only learn.

Many a child has grown up with no confidence in himself
because his parents would not allow him to do things for himself.
Such a situation need not exist, however. We can enhance and
fortify a child's confidence by showing some trust and interest in
him. Isn't that what God does to us, his children? God says, "Here

is my world which I have made for you. You are my ambassadors in it. Go tame it and claim it." The thought that God would entrust his creation to the likes of me is a stroke to my ego and a boost to my confidence. It helps me to feel about myself the way a young boy who delivered groceries part-time felt about himself. He went to the home of a new customer with her order. She asked his name. "Humphrey Bogart," he answered proudly. His customer replied, "Well, that's a pretty well-known name." Without a moment's hesitation he said, "It should be. I've been delivering groceries around here for four years." Andrew Gillies probably had someone like him in mind when he wrote "Two Prayers."

> Last night my little boy confessed to me
> Some childish wrong;
> And kneeling at my knee,
> He prayed with tears—
> "Dear God, make me a man
> Like Daddy—wise and strong;
> I know you can.
>
> Then while he slept
> I knelt beside his bed,
> Confessed my sins,
> And prayed with low-bowed head.
> "O God, make me a child
> Like my child here—
> Pure, guileless,
> Trusting Thee with faith sincere."[2]

Confidence, openness, positive effects on others—these reasons show us why Jesus chose youngsters to be symbols of salvation.

Holy Father, we are your children, regardless of our ages. Make us young at heart so our love isn't hampered by spiritual "hardening of the arteries." In the name, power, and purpose of Him who loves children, Amen.

# 2

# He Took a Coin

*Matthew 22:15-22*

Jesus took a coin—or was it a mirror? In either case he showed his questioners how easily they could see themselves in the coins they held. In that case the very item they held actually held them. How I love the way Jesus' mind worked. He was fully aware that the Pharisees were in no sense interested in his real thoughts and feelings. Their only concern was catching Jesus in their snare. But as is often the case, they fell into their own trap.

This story demonstrates that Jesus and his questioners were not even on the same wavelength. Have you ever tried to talk with someone who was not genuinely interested in what you had to say? If so, then you can understand why Jesus used the symbolism of a coin in an attempt to communicate his message. The Pharisees only wanted Jesus to speak the wrong words just once so they could haul him into court for treason and blasphemy. The question was tricky—a "have-you-stopped-beating-your-wife?" question. Jesus simply could not answer "yes" or "no." The dice were loaded against him. So Jesus took a coin, and when he did the battle was as good as over. All money of that day was considered property of the emperor. It carried his image. He allowed the citizens the privilege of using it, but there was a catch. As soon as they accepted the money they also accepted the emperor's rule over them. They took Caesar's coins but had to give their allegiance in return.

There are no right answers to wrong questions. The Pharisees had asked the wrong question. It should not have been, "Jesus, shall we pay?" but, "Jesus, shall we give allegiance and priority to Caesar or to God?" The question behind the question was, "Do we, like these coins, have the emperor's image stamped on us, or do we have God's image on us?"

Persons are like coins—each minted separately, some almost perfect, others flawed, but all worth something. The Bible teaches us that we are made in the image of God. Among other ideas, this truth means that we are not mere animals. We are related to God, for he is our Father (and I can also safely say, our Mother through redemption in Christ). The prophet Ezekiel noted the Lord as saying, "The life of every person belongs to me" (18:4). While this is true, we must remember that human beings live in the tension of freedom. We must choose whether or not to live up to our relationship to God. We shall be sons and daughters or prodigals. The Book of Deuteronomy pictures Moses forcing the Hebrews to decide which course of action would be theirs: "Today I am giving you a choice between a blessing and a curse—a blessing if you obey the commandments of the Lord your God that I am giving you today, but a curse, if you disobey these commands and turn away to worship other gods that you have never worshipped before" (11:26-28, TEV).

From one perspective, the entire Bible is a saga of the inevitable choice faced by the Hebrews and the early Christians. Moses answered the question, "Shall we give priority to the Lord or to something else?" Adam and Eve faced this question in the Garden of Eden, and we all know the consequences of their choice. Elijah confronted the prophets of Baal on Mount Carmel and piercingly asked, "How much longer will it take you to make up your minds? If the Lord is God, worship him; but if Baal is God, worship him!" Job had to choose whether to bless God or to curse him.

Jesus faced temptations in the wilderness, temptations real

enough to have destroyed his ministry had he chosen wrong. He chose to obey God rather than the tempter. And us? Everyone of us also must choose our priorities—God or money? God or pleasure? God or hollow respectability? Even when we choose God, we must be certain our choice is the real God and not a saccharin substitute. Martha Foote Crowe has a poem entitled "The Wooden Christ," in which she envisions an army marching past a wooden statue of Jesus.

> At the high ridge
> Of a wide war-stricken realm
> There stands an ancient wooden Christ.
> Hollow the tottering image towers,
> Eyeless, and rotten, and decrepit there,
> His smile a cruel twist.
> Within the empty heart of this old Christ
> Small stinging insects build their nests;
> And iron-hearted soldiers cross themselves
> The while they pass
> The hollow-hearted figure by.
>
> I think there is no Christ left there
> In all those carnage-loving lands
> Save only this of hollow wood
> With wasp nests
> Hiving in its heart.[1]

I must admit that more than once have I chosen a "hollow-hearted Christ" over the real one.

The Pharisees were befuddled when Jesus turned the question around against them. He asked, "To whom do you belong, to Caesar or to God?" Caught off guard, they had no answer. If they said "Caesar," the people would have been outraged. If they answered "God," then Jesus would have asked why they did not do God's will. In a sense he said, "Listen, you people had better straighten out your priorities."

The point of the conflict between Jesus and the Pharisees is easy to miss. They were interested in preserving their religious tradition from the onslaughts of paganism. This was actually a worthy motive, but they carried their efforts to extremes. In their effort to protect God they actually kept him at arms distance. One of the ironies of religious life generally is that we sometimes blind ourselves staring at the light. A Hindu once asked a Christian why he sought God with his eyes closed in prayer. He urged the Christian to see God with his eyes open—in the form of the poor, the starved, the illiterate, and the afflicted. This would have been good council for the Pharisees. But, in truth, we are their spiritual descendants. I am reminded of a parody penned by some unknown sage:

> Once there was a Christian,
>    He had a pious look;
> His consecration was complete—
>    Except his pocketbook.
>
> He'd put a nickel in the plate,
>    And then with might and main
> He'd sing, "When we assunder part
>    It gives us inward pain."

All have blinders. All need more sight and insight, not just the Pharisees of Jesus' day.

*1. Jesus took a coin—like all money, a symbol of ownership.* Caesar's image was stamped on the coin showing it belonged to him. The proverb, "Whoever's mark is on you, his you are," is true today as it was two millennia ago. The Kiowa Indians used to be able to tell their arrows from those of all other tribes. The braves would chew the shafts to straighten them, so good Kiowa Indian arrows had tooth marks on them. I am not stretching the analogy too far when I suggest that we have the marks of ownership on us. The question for us to answer is, "Whose marks are they?" I recently met a sophisticated pagan. She seemed to have it made and lived her life with no reference to God. She had identification marks indelibly tatooed on her attitude. But they do not satisfy and only leave empty longings in the heart. Morris Bishop noted the absurdity of giving full allegiance to any strictly secular enterprise. He showed what happens to our personalities in such an offer. Bishop did all of this in his funny story-poem, "The Perforated Spirit."

> The fellows up in Personnel,
>     They have a set of cards on me.
> The sprinkled perforations tell
>     My individuality.
>
> And what am I? I am a chart
>     Upon the cards of IBM;
> The secret places of the heart
>     Have little secrecy for them.
>
> It matters not how I may prate,
>     They punch with punishments my scroll.
> The files are masters of my fate,
>     They are the captains of my soul.
>
> Monday my brain began to buzz;
>     I was in agony all night.
> I found out what the trouble was:
>     They had my paper clip too tight.[2]

Is this not a true reflection of our status if we place all our trust in gadgets instead of God? As Jules Bertillon put it, it leaves us "sitting in a shower of gold, with nothing to hold up but a pitchfork."

Sooner or later everyone must answer the question, "To whom or what do you belong?" A tragedy of our time is that many people think the golden age comes only with God. They agree with Oscar Wilde who once quipped, "When I was young I thought that money was the most important thing in life; now that I am old I *know* that it is." The genius of the Christian faith is that it helps us to transcend the power of possessions. While they lock us to things and time,

God helps us place our priorities on higher things, especially God himself. Things in general and money in particular are not necessarily evil, but they can be. If we spend our money foolishly we forfeit the chance to use it for positive causes. I thoroughly disagree with Billy Rose who advised against investing your money in anything that eats or needs repairing. People fit both categories!

2. *Give God priority—but why?* In all the causes and items vying for dedication, why should we give ourselves to God and his church? To many persons these seem last on the list of important matters. Someone asks, "Why should I believe in God when science provides everything I need?" The question must be moved back a couple of steps. Who created science and scientists? Who so ordered this universe that it operates with schedule and predictability? Who allowed researchers to discover that predictability and name it "scientific law"? Science can synthesize many loose and seemingly unrelated facts and develop theories. But it cannot give meaning to life or create beauty or love. Richard Armour once heard a speech given before the members of the New York State Frozen Food Locker Association. The speaker told his audience that their frozen food lockers were good places to hide in the event of a nuclear explosion. Radiation supposedly would not leak into the locker. Armour reflected his feeling for that idea in a little poem:

> Move over, ham
>     And quartered cow,
> My Geiger says
>     The time is now.
>
> Yes, now I lay me
>     Down to sleep,
> And if I die,
>     At least I'll keep.[3]

Perhaps our best of science could "keep" us, but it cannot make us want to live. Money cannot do it either. It is only a mutually agreed-upon symbol of worth. As a symbol it can change at any time. Have you tried to buy any gold lately, or pay your bills with Confederate currency? Besides that, many people have noticed that money seems to change the people who supposedly own it. Vic Oliver, for example, said that if a man runs after it, he's money-mad. If he keeps it, he's a capitalist; if he spends it, he's a playboy; if he doesn't get it, he's a ne'er-do-well; if he doesn't try to get it, he lacks ambition. If he gets it without working for it, he's a parasite; and if he accumulates it after a lifetime of hard work, people call him a fool who never got anything out of life.[4]

Wealth is fickle and has no power to tame a restless heart. Think of Elvis Presley or Howard Hughes. Jesus used a coin to teach his critics that they must not give themselves to money, but to God. And it must be a giving of everything. E. Stanley Jones once stayed in a hotel with the following sign in his room: "Please turn the radiator all the way on or all the way off. If they are turned partially on they are noisy and leak." I can't help but feel this is a parable of religious commitment—all the way on or all the way off! Revelation 3:15-16 pictures the angel of the church in Laodicea saying, "I know that you are neither cold nor hot. How I wish you were either one or the other! But because you are lukewarm, neither hot nor cold, I am going to spit you out of my mouth!" (TEV).

The journey toward putting God in first place is tough, especially when the path seems booby-trapped. Everybody seems to have their hands out for a cut from our lives.

Even our best intentions are severely tested. We decide to follow God completely and then, before we know it, we get sidetracked again. Winston Churchill was once in a hurry to reach the BBC studio in London for a speech. When he hailed a cab and told of his destination the driver said, "Sorry, I can't go that far and still be home in an hour. You see, Churchill is addressing the country, and I don't want to miss it." The prime minister was so moved that he gave the driver a pound note out of gratitude. The would-be listener grabbed the money and said, "A pound?! To blazes with Churchill. Hop in."

With all of these stones along the path to trip us, and the traps to snare us, how can we give first priority to God?

3. *Remember that all things outside of God are transient.* This means that we cannot give the eternal longings of our hearts to anything except God and be satisfied. As Alfred Lord Tennyson put it:

> Our little systems have their day;
> They have their day and cease to be;
> They are but broken lights of thee;
> And thou, O Lord, are more than they.

The ancient Romans vowed to build a society which would last for millennia. But they're gone. Hitler promised the Third Reich would last a thousand years. It was dead and buried in less than twenty. Caesar's image was on the coins of the Pharisees. He is dead and his coins lost to oblivion. We cannot give our lives fully to something or someone which can't last. Would you build a house of cotton candy? No person, no government, no way of life is permanent but one—the kingdom of God and its Lord. To invest in anything less is tragic. I think I now understand the Chinese proverb which says, "He who sacrifices his conscience to ambition burns a picture to obtain the ashes." I admit that I live with many ashes because I put other things before God.

Marilee Zdenek expressed this idea in a prayer entitled, "Renewal."

> You asked for my hands that You could use them for Your purpose.
> I gave them for a moment and then withdrew when the work was hard.
> You asked for a mouth to speak out against injustice.
> I gave you a whisper that I might not be accused.
> You asked for my eyes that I might see the pain of poverty.
> I closed them for I did not want to know.
> You asked for my life that You might work through me.

I gave you a fractional part that I might not get involved.
Lord, forgive me, renew me, and send me out as a usable instrument
That I may take seriously the meaning of Your cross.[5]

Now what shall we do? Can we fashion our lives with no
reference to God? If we do we will be like the man who told his
psychologist, "Every time I get my act together the curtain comes
down." Historian Will Durant once said that the greatest question
of our time is not communism versus individualism, not Europe
versus America, not even the East versus the West: it is whether
man can bear to live without God.

I agree with Durant. We can talk about our beliefs and
commitments all we want to, but our actions must give credence to
our words. Aesop tells of a groom who would steal the grain
intended for the horse and, without his master's knowledge, sell it
in the village. But all day long he kept very busy grooming and
currying the horse. "If you really are so anxious that I look well,"
said the horse one day to his groom, "then give me less of your
brushing and more of your corn."

Jesus took a coin, and in so doing invited us to give God priority
in our lives. As someone put it, "You can't stand everywhere, not
even if you twist and spin like a weathervane. You can't stand
nowhere; you have to live by some faith. . . . You can't stand
anywhere for one faith obviously is not as fine as another. You and I
have to stand somewhere. With Christ? Is there any braver place?"

# 3

# He Took the Hand of a Sick Child

*Matthew 9:18-26*

On hearing the slogan, "God is dead," a California pastor asked, "If that's true, then why wasn't I notified? I'm a member of the family." I laughed when I heard him relate this story, but as is often the case with humor, a profound truth was presented. This man *is* a part of the family of God. He has millions of brothers and sisters, too. Countless others are wondering how they can be properly related to God.

Jesus came to show how we can live our lives in correct standing with God. In fact, the word "salvation" in the Bible often conveys the concept of relationships which are set right. The incident of Jesus' taking the hand of a sick child in Matthew 9 portrays one aspect of salvation—wholesome relationships.

The focus of this chapter is symbolized in Jesus' agreement to make a journey to heal a child. Along the way he was detoured shortly, but even the delay was a teaching device. With these thoughts in mind we can ask, "How do we relate to God?"

*1. Be real with God.* American Christianity is plagued by the myth that somehow Christians are to be all smiles and no trouble. But we *do* have problems and should admit this fact. Instead of playing games with God, acknowledge the concern. The official who sought Jesus was playing no game. The life of his daughter was on the line and he was serious. The sin of Ananias and Sapphira as described in Acts 5 is that of playing games. They felt that they could pretend to be what they were not. They withheld not only their money but themselves. The results were tragic.

Be real and honest with yourself and God. Playwright Herb Gardner has a character in one of his plays who tries to protect his nephew from becoming "one of the nice dead people," that is, one who simply flows along in life, never questioning or probing. The man wants to keep his nephew from becoming a "Norman Nothing." Being truthful with God is never easy, but unless we are, we stand the possibilities of becoming "nice dead people," or ostriches with our heads in the sand. Sir Henry Alford once said, "Truth does not consist in minute accuracy of detail, but in conveying the right impression."

Christians sometimes assume that God does not want to hear our heart-felt problems. But our assumptions about God are often wrong. J. B. Phillips once asked a group of children during World War II if they believed God understood radar. They answered "No." Phillips points out that many people, not merely children, assume God is a kindly old gentleman who is rather bewildered with modern progress. We do not help God's cause when we think and speak of him in this fashion. God is always greater than even our best assumptions about him. He wants us to acknowledge the real concerns of our lives to him in prayer. This is what I mean about being truthful with God. Albert E. Day wrote that someone once told him, "Albert, you tell so many unnecessary truths." Day pointed out that the man was not challenging the truth of what he (Day) said. Instead the man was indicating that truth is not always welcome. Day says, "We are not living morally unless we welcome, in fact, run out to meet, truth whatever its source or the changes it demands in our thinking and practice. . . . " Day continues, "Faith that lives in fear of truth is not faith but faithlessness."[1] I agree totally and am reminded of the oft-repeated proverb: "Fear knocked on the door; faith answered; no one was there."

Be truthful with God about the sorrow you hear in life. Too often we assume that sorrow is a sign of divine disfavor. Like Job of ancient days, problems are simply equated with sin. But Jesus declared that *all* his followers would carry heavy burdens. Real religion is not a way to escape sorrow, but rather a means of enduring it and triumphing over it. The Jews have an ancient legend of the "Sorrow Tree." According to this legend, on the day of judgment each person will be allowed to hang all of his unhappiness on a branch of the great tree. Each person then will walk around the tree and examine all of the troubles hanging in the branches. Anyone may freely choose those of someone else. But, as the legend concludes, each person chooses to reclaim his own personal set of sorrows rather than those of others. Each person leaves the "Sorrow Tree" wiser than when he came.

The man who asked Jesus to come heal his daughter was truthful about the sorrow he carried. Had he not been, I feel sure that Jesus would not have gone with him, and we probably never would have heard of this incident. Jesus knew that the reality of his situation could break the man's heart and courage. The man had to face reality, as many people who preceded, and also followed, him have done. On July 11, 1840, Elizabeth Barrett Browning's brother, Edward, drowned. She wrote a poem, "De Profundis," which ends as follows:

> The heart which like a staff was one
> For mine to lean and rest upon;
> The strongest on the longest day
> With steadfast love is caught away,
> And yet my days go on, go on.

You can almost feel the heartbreak in this poem, especially in the last line. Yet, Mrs. Browning is a good example of facing sorrow truthfully. Another of her poems, "Substitution," expresses what faith can do in the face of tragedy.

> When some beloved voice that was to you
> Both sound and sweetness, faith suddenly,

And silence, against which you dare not cry,
Aches around you like a strong disease and new—
What hope? What help? What music will undo
That silence to your sense? Not friendship's sigh,
Not reasons subtle count. . . .
Not songs of poets, nor of nightingales . . . Nay, none of these,
Speak *thou*, availing Christ!—and fill this pause.

Being "up front" with our feelings allows us to learn and profit from our experiences. As Robert Browning Hamilton put it,

I walked a mile with Pleasure;
    She chatted all the way;
But left me none the wiser
    For all she had to say.

I walked a mile with Sorrow,
    And ne'er a word said she;
But, oh! the things I lear'nt from her,
    When Sorrow walked with me.[2]

2. *Be patient with people.* That Jesus would stop on his way to the official's house to speak with a sick woman is one of the surprises of this story. I wonder if I had been in Jesus' place what would have happened. The scene would probably have been something like this: "Now, madam, I can certainly sympathize with your circumstances, and I'm sure you need some help. But right now I'm late for a meeting at the church so I've gotta' run. I'll be praying for you, though." How tragic when we use our religion as an excuse to escape helping those in need. But it happens all the time. Do you remember Jesus' parable about the good Samaritan?

Chickens come about by hatching eggs, not by smashing them open with a rock. Teeth are straightened through the patient persistence of an orthodontist's care. Can you imagine what would happen if he tried to do it like a carpenter who straightens nails with a crowbar and hammer? Patience in all things concerning people is a *must*. All of us are imperfect and need understanding. I once took classical guitar lessons for a few months. Since I had taught myself to play in incorrect style before my lessons, my teacher had to *unteach* me before he could teach me. I still recall how upset he would get when he would watch me play with my incorrect, self-taught fingering. He worked hard at being patient with me but he often failed.

Christianity tells us that we must be patient with other people. The biblical word "longsuffering" conveys this idea. When we fail, problems always arise. Aesop told the story of a young man who hired an ass and a driver to take him from Athens to Megara one hot summer day. The sun's heat was so scorching at midday that, feeling faint, the man dismounted to rest himself in the shadow of the beast. The driver began to argue with the young man that he had equal claim to the shadow. "What!" exclaimed the youth. "Didn't I hire this ass for the whole journey?" "Yes, indeed," said the driver, "you hired this beast but not his shadow." And while the two were wrangling, the ass took to his heels and ran away. You see, more than one argument has nothing but a shadow for a basis!

When Jesus stopped for the woman who touched him in a crowd he was reflecting the attitude God always has toward his children. Hosea the prophet mirrored God's patience in these words:

> How can I give you up, Israel?
> How can I abandon you? Could I
> ever destroy you as I did Admah,
> or treat you as I did Zeboim?
> My heart will not let me do it!
> My love for you is too strong.

(11:8, TEV)

Just why the Lord is so patient with us I cannot hope to understand. But I do think he sometimes feels like the man who was walking through a supermarket with his screaming baby in his shopping cart. A woman nearby noticed that from time to time he would calmly say, "Keep calm, Albert. Keep calm, Albert." In admiration for his patience as the child continued to wail, the woman walked up to him and said, "Sir, I must commend you for your patience with baby Albert." At this the man looked her squarely in the eye and replied, "Lady, *I* am Albert!"

Paul asked the Roman Christians, "Do you think you will escape God's judgment? Or perhaps you despise his great kindness, tolerance, and patience. Surely you know that God is kind because he is trying to lead you to repent." (2:3-4, TEV). Longfellow wrote,

> Though the mills of God grind slowly,
> yet they grind exceedingly small;
> Though with patience He stands waiting,
> with exactness grinds He all.

The Lord is patient with us. Return the favor.

*3. Be suspicious of the obvious.* In this Scripture passage, Jesus was laughed at for attending the official's daughter. Why? It was because the neighbors knew that life had already left her. She was *obviously dead.* Everybody knew it and the professional mourners had been called in. But Jesus challenged this assumption with both words and actions. He did that often in his ministry. Everyone knew that no prophet could come from Nazareth. But one did. Everyone knew that no Jew could care for non-Jews. But one did. Everybody knew that no one could ever be greater than Abraham, Isaac, and Jacob. But one was. Everyone knew the child was dead. But one was not yet ready to put her in the grave.

Obvious truths can be real burdens to progress. Think of how many great things have been done by people who have been suspicious of the obvious. At one time most people said, "The earth is flat." But Ferdinand Magellan didn't believe it, so he sailed around the world. The ancient Greeks proclaimed, "Water is the essence of all matter and life." But others were suspicious and discovered essences such as DNA molecules. Only fifty years ago people said, "Man will never set foot on the moon." But we all

know what happened on a summer's day in 1969. Alfred North
Whitehead once opined, "It requires a very unusual mind to
undertake an analysis of the obvious." I agree. We can "miss the
forest for the trees" in obvious matters.

I recently got a haircut from a particularly talkative barber. He
spoke with great authority how World War III was coming soon. I
asked him how he knew and he answered, "*Everybody* knows. It's
obvious." I shot back, "I'm a somebody and I don't know it." He
finished clipping my hair in sulking silence. We don't like our
"knowledge" and opinions disapproved of or challenged. But for
our own good, some of them must be challenged. For example,
smoking was seen as an "in" thing to do only a few years ago. But
recent information shows that this seemingly safe pastime is
extremely hazardous.

A poor widow living alone in the country kept a favorite hen.
Each morning this hen laid a big, brown egg for the woman's
breakfast. One day the widow thought, "If I were to double my
hen's allowance of barley, she would lay two eggs a day instead of
one." So she started feeding her biddy a double measure of grain,
and soon the hen began to grow fat and lazy. Not long afterwards
she stopped laying altogether! An "obvious" conclusion was wrong.
Sometimes it is quite the opposite.

In 1945 Charles Kaman conceived the idea that all guitars did
not have to look as they had for hundreds of years. Kaman founded
a corporation and began designing a different style of instrument.
The first of these, known as Ovation guitars, hit the market in
1967. People laughed at first because they had bowed backs
instead of flat backs. Today Kaman is laughing. His company did
about $ 326 million in business in 1979.

Isn't religion actually a belief in the not-so-obvious in the face of
the obvious? Hebrew 11:1 in *The New English Bible* reads, "And
what is faith? Faith gives substance to our hopes, and makes us
certain of the realities we do not see." The official in Matthew 9

believed that his daughter had died. But he hoped beyond hope that Jesus could do something. The lesson is that we relate to God in such a manner that, whatever comes our way, we will not be crushed.

Jesus took the hand of a sick child. In doing so he symbolized reality, patience, and belief in truth which was beyond the obvious. Phillips Brooks wrote, "Christianity knows no truth which is not the child of love and the parent of duty." God's salvation is exactly that kind of truth. Let us accept it.

# 4

# He Took His Closest Friends

*Matthew 26:36-46*

Someone I consider a close friend recently betrayed my trust in him. Even as I pen these words the memory of that betrayal is painful. I forgive him, though. I have to, because I have betrayed others' trust in me. It might seem simpler not to have friends at all. That way no one could get close to me and hurt me. That is a luxury reserved only for my imagination, however. While I do occasionally get hurt by friends, I receive joy and love most of the time. You see, I *need* my friends.

We are sometimes surprised to learn that even Jesus needed friends. We seem to think of him as something of a "Lone Ranger" who prowled around Palestine with only a dozen "Tontos." Jesus had friends, many of them. You will recall that his first miracle was at the wedding feast of a friend. He laughed with those who were joyous, and he wept when a good friend, Lazarus, died.

Our choice of friends speaks volumes about us. Cervantes says in *Don Quixote*, "Tell me what company thou keepest, and I'll tell thee what thou art." Consider testimony from other writers who have discovered this truth. Oliver Goldsmith penned, "Good company upon the road, said the proverb, is the shortest cut." Jeremy Taylor observed, "No man can be provident of his time that is not prudent in the choice of his company." Lessing stated it as follows:

> The most agreeable of all companions is a simple, frank man, without
> any high pretensions to an oppressive greatness; one who loves life, and

> understands the use of it; obliging alike at all hours; above all, of a golden temper and steadfast as an anchor. For such a one we gladly exchange the greatest genius, the most brilliant wit, the profoundest thinker.

Jesus knew this to be true, as did Matthew, who recorded the incident for us. We can glean three truths from this account of the friendship between Jesus and the three other men. The first concerns

1. *The need for support.* With remarkable candor Matthew relates that Jesus took his three closest friends into the garden for support as He made the most important decision of his life. What were Peter, James, and John to Jesus? We cannot be sure of all the details but this much is clear: they were close, trusted men who shared Jesus' ecstasy of spiritual fulfillment and agony of his spiritual pilgrimage.

When he prayed in the garden for strength to give all to the Father, it was no sham battle. He was "sorrowful and troubled," as Matthew put it. He needed his friends exactly as we need ours when we hurt. I am sure that the three were to Jesus what others were to the Quaker William Penn. In his spiritual classic, *Fruits of Solitude*, Penn wisely observed, "A true friend unbosoms freely, advises justly, assists readily, adventures boldly, takes all patiently, defends courageously, and continues a friend unchangeably."

The Old Testament has several accounts of persons who were highly supportive of each other. Second Kings 10:15 relates how Jehu and Jehonadab linked their hearts in support of each other. Jehu "greeted [him] and said to him, 'Is your heart true to my heart as mine is to yours?' And Jehonadab answered, 'It is.'" (RSV). Who could forget the account of God speaking to Moses in Exodus 33:11? "Thus the Lord used to speak to Moses face to face, as a man speaks to his friend." Sometimes we are lonely because we will not allow anyone to care for us. "To have a friend, be a friend" advises an old proverb. It could be rephrased to read, "To have a friend, allow yourself to have one."

"No man is an island, complete unto himself," not even Jesus. So he took his friends because he needed their support. The poet Cowper, in realization and appreciation of great friendship, wrote to Heskith: "You must know that I should not love you half so much did I not know that you would be my friend for all eternity. There is not room for friendship to unfold itself in such a little nook of life as this."

A friend is someone who is "in place" for us. That is, he or she is where they need to be in relation to us. For example, I am thinking of a close friend who knows when to be close and when to give me room. Because we are friends, he is not offended if I show or tell him I need some solitude and space. We care for each other so we try to be "in place" for each other. Milton Meyeroff has a fascinating book entitled *On Caring*, in which he says:

> We are "in place" in the world through having our lives ordered by inclusive caring. This is in contrast with being "out of place," trying to escape from the "wrong place," seeking one's "place," and indifference and insensitivity to "place." It is not as though a preexistent place were waiting for us; we are not in place as coins are in a box, but rather we both find and make our place in the same way in which the person who "finds" himself must have helped to "create" himself as well.[1]

Obvious from Meyeroff's analysis is the fact that hard work is required to be a friend! He goes on to note some of the major ingredients of caring in friendship: knowing, patience, honesty, trust, humility, hope, and courage. No wonder we have so few *close* friends. When we study the encounters which Jesus had with people, we are often attracted to the fact that his encounters were anything but shallow. He invested himself in relationships. He was "present." I once tried to talk with a "star," but he made it painfully obvious that while his body was in front of me, he was in reality far away in thoughts. I terminated the conversation because I do not like being treated as a "necessary evil" in the life of a famous person.

Sometimes people try too hard to be our friends. They seem to smother us rather than giving us room to grow and mature. Healthy persons need room and freedom to grow. Those who almost breathe down our necks could actually stunt our growth. This fact is hard to learn, especially for teenagers. A group of three or four may "pal around" together for years, but as they reach mid- to late-teen years, things change. One or more persons may withdraw from the group and seek a new direction for himself or herself. This can be natural and healthy, but those left behind may see this person as "snooty" or "stuck up."

True friendship requires that we be sensitive to each other's needs. If one of those needs is to move in another direction, then bless that person and let him or her go. This benefits not only the other but also ourselves. The only way we can be mature is to allow the other person that same freedom. Milton Meyeroff also put it this way:

> In order to live "my own life" I must make it my own through caring and taking responsibility for it, just as I must act on an idea and help to actualize it if I am to make it on my own. I am not autonomous to begin with; autonomy is an achievement like maturity or the growth of a significant friendship.[2] . . . Autonomy does not mean doing anything I please; in caring for my appropriate others I do not act arbitrarily. How and what I do are significantly determined by what is required of me by my others if they are to grow and be actualized, and by my own needs to grow. Although my direction is largely determined by the growth of others, I experience myself as the initiator of my acts and as responsible for my own life, and not simply as acted on and controlled from outside. Direction emerges within my life, instead of being something predetermined or forced on me from outside. Autonomy is the opposite of both arbitrary behavior (doing simply as I please) and behavior controlled by what is basically foreign to me.[3]

Jesus needed the support of his friends, even as we need it from ours and they from us. But we cannot be controlled by them nor can we control them. Oscar Wilde once said, "To love one's self is the beginning of a lifelong romance." Too many of us indulge in this affection! Greek mythology has the story of Narcissus, a handsome youth who saw the reflection of himself in a pool. He gradually pined away as he looked longingly at his own reflection. If we love only ourselves we will have no real friends for loving support. A biography of a rock music star tells of her selfish, despicable attitudes toward others. She died rich but friendless.

Salvation in the New Testament is described as completeness. Human life is simply incomplete without healthy relationships with other people as well as God. Jesus took his three close friends. He needed their support. They needed his.

A second aspect is:

2. *The tragedy of neglect.* "He came to the disciples and found them sleeping." Fiction's Rip van Winkle gained his fame by sleeping through a revolution. But he was preceded by three men and nearly two millennia! Peter, James, and John missed the revolution of a man struggling to submit all of his life to God. Jesus was a real human being, just as you and I. He was and is God—but also man. No normal person *wants* to die. Jesus did not either, but he knew that he must obey God, regardless of the outcome.

Keith Parks, executive secretary of the Foreign Mission Board of the Southern Baptist Convention, tells of a missionary who was killed in Rhodesia (now called Zimbabwe). Other American missionaries in that area were understandably nervous. Two of them, a doctor and wife, were struggling to keep a small hospital open. Asked if they wanted to leave, they said, "No! If we close it more will die than will die if we stay and keep it open. Some things in life are still worth dying for."

Jesus knew this truth and resolved to battle for it, even if his closest friends failed to understand and help. They were the ones, however, who missed the opportunity to walk with Jesus through his "valley of the shadow of death." Neglect brings rust to exposed metal, overheating to a car's engine not properly cooled, fraying to clothing not maintained, and atrophy to one's soul.

No one wants to be neglected, whether it be Jesus or anyone else. Winston Churchill once noted that politicians become used to being caricatured. He said, "If we must confess it, they are often offended and downcast when the cartoons stop. . . . They fear old age and obsolescence are creeping upon them. They murmur: 'We are not mauled and maltreated as we used to be. The great days are gone.'"

We commonly neglect God by disregarding the deep things of his Spirit within our lives. We like to be suave and urbane, keeping our "cool" in all circumstances, maintaining neutrality on all issues. Was this the problem of Jesus' friends? Dante once noted, "The hottest places in hell are reserved for those who, in a time of great moral crisis, maintain their neutrality." When I am honest with myself I admit that I understand Peter, James, and John. I'm so much like them, neglecting the things of God while pursuing personal interests, of which spiritual sleep is but one.

Many people today have difficulty understanding this incident because they forget that Jesus was, as the early church later called him, "fully God, fully man." His humanity is transparent in this passage of Scripture. He was struggling with God in the garden, just as his spiritual ancestor, Jacob, struggled with an angel at Jabbok. Both were unrelenting. Jesus struggled with God. The disciples struggled only with dreams. Is it really so mysterious that they misunderstood?

Jesus tended to the call of his soul's deepest needs. For this some ridiculed him for being "impractical" while praising the disciples for resting before a hard day ahead. But our sense of what is "practical" often causes us problems. William Butler Yeats wrote, "Why should we honor those that die upon the field of battle; a man may show as much reckless courage in entering into the abyss of himself." That night in the garden was Jesus' time of entering that abyss. But his friends missed it. If you had been there could you have stayed awake?

A third aspect is:

3. *The hope of surrender.* To many a human eye the mission of Jesus was an abysmal failure. Matthew records that a mob seized Jesus in the garden and led him away to be tried for treason. But what happened before his arrest turned the tide? He surrendered his will to God's will. It was *the* decisive moment in his life and in the future of all mankind. Jesus *could* have escaped during the night. He *could* have bribed a mob to protect him. He *could* have called on twelve legions of angels to help, but he chose to stand by his integrity and, for lack of a better term, "let the chips fall where they may." For all his mighty teaching and preaching, Jesus' life would have failed totally had he not surrendered to God that night. Thinking of his decision to stay, Edwin Prince Booth wrote, "A word unsupported by life is lost upon the wind. A word supported by a life is incarnated into history." And so it is. We know Jesus today because he answered "yes" to the Father. Luke says that "his sweat became like great drops of blood falling down upon the ground." Was he not saying, "By the sweat of your heart shall you earn your dignity"?

In his monumental "In Memoriam," Tennyson set the issue in perspective:

> Perplext in faith, but pure in deeds,
>     At last he beat his music out.
>     There lives more faith in honest doubt,
> Believe me, than in half the creeds.
>
> He fought his doubts and gather'd strength,
>     He would not make his judgment blind,
>     He faced the specters of the mind
> And laid them; thus he came at length.

To find a stronger faith his own
    And Power was with him in the night,
    Which makes the darkness and the light,
And dwells not in the light alone.

So Jesus battled in the night, and emerged through his surrender
to his Father. Hanging in the balance was more than his own
destiny, but also that of the whole world. Sidney Lanier captured
this truth in "A Ballad of Trees and the Master."

Into the woods my Master went,
Clean forspent, forspent.
Into the woods my Master came,
Forspent with love and shame.
But the olives they were not blind to Him,
The little gray leaves were kind to Him:
The thorn-tree had a mind to Him
When into the woods He came.

Out of the woods my Master went,
And He was well content.
Out of the woods my Master came,
Content with death and shame.
When Death and Shame would woo Him last,
From under the trees they drew Him last:
'Twas on a tree they slew Him—last
When out of the woods He came.

Our salvation comes by way of Jesus' absolute surrender to God.
Yet the scene in the garden is repeated in miniature when each of
us says "yes" to the claim of God upon our lives. We must also give
over to God all that we have, good and bad. For example, a friend of
mine is a talented musician but must give that talent to God in
order to truly make it count. Another friend and his wife recently
had a child which lived for only thirty-two days. They received a
bill from the hospital for $42,000! He said, "Don, it's like going to
a carnival, spending $42,000, and then leaving without even

having a teddy bear to take home." They must surrender that crushing grief to God in order to get over it.

Aesop told of a proud oak tree which stood for 100 years but was finally blown over by a storm. It fell into a river and was carried downstream, coming to rest on a bank where some reeds were growing. Amazed, the oak asked, "How did you weather that storm? It was too powerful even for me, but you are still here." "That's just it," replied the reeds. "All these years you have stubbornly pitted your great strength against the wind. You were too proud to yield a little. We, on the other hand, just bend and let the wind blow over us without trying to resist it. The harder the wind blows, the more we humble ourselves, so here I am!"

This aptly illustrates our surrender to the all-embracing will of God. For God demands of us what Ulysses S. Grant demanded in a letter to General S. B. Buckner during the Civil War: "No terms except an immediate and unconditional surrender can be accepted."

Jesus took his friends. He needed them then, and he needs them now. They let him down, just as we do. But ours is a loving and forgiving Lord. He shows us how to give our lives to him who multiplies their usefulness a thousandfold.

# 5

# He Took a Towel

*John 13:1-17*

"He took a towel." Jesus? God on his knees? Was this whole scene like a frame from an old movie? You know the kind. The hero assumes the role of the humblest member of the cast, does his magnificent feat that saves the day, and of course wins the affections of the prettiest girl. Did it really look like that? Probably not.

Jesus was not an ancient Errol Flynn, seeking his own aggrandizement at the expense of others. When he picked up a towel Jesus was symbolizing one of the major elements of salvation—service. The washing of his disciples' feet was Jesus' way of saying, "*No one* is too good to serve others. Just as I do it to you, so you are to do this for others."

John informs us that Jesus knew he was about to be betrayed. There were "wolves among the sheep." Yet even in the shroud of treason, Jesus was still interested in serving his friends. He loved them and gave himself in humble service. In his book, *Peace of Mind,* Joshua Liebman wrote, "We discover that rigid pride is actually the supreme foe of inner victory, while flexible humility, the kind of humility that appears when we do not demand the impossible or the angelic of ourselves, is the great ally of psychic peace."[1]

Many are blocked from spiritual peace by this "rigid pride." Yet giving in is the only avenue to real victory. I can speak with authority on both accounts. At times I am so filled with destructive pride that no one, not even God, can seem to teach me. The Bible often calls this being "stiff-necked." The image is of a person too proud to bow his head before the Lord. At other times (not often enough, I'm afraid) I feel flexible and malleable. God cannot mold hard clay, but he does work with soft, pliable material. When I give myself to him, God uses all the gifts he has given me for his service.

In one of his most autobiographical works, *De Profundis*, Oscar Wilde spoke with unusual candor and power about this situation. Although this quotation is rather long, consider his council:

> I bore up against everything with some stubbornness of will and much rebellion of nature, till I had absolutely nothing left in the world but one thing. I had lost my name, my position, my happiness, my freedom, my wealth. I was a prisoner and a pauper. But I still had my children left. Suddenly they were taken away from me by the law. It was a blow so appalling that I did not know what to do, so I flung myself on my knees, and bowed my head, and wept, and said, "The body of a child is as the body of the Lord: I am not worthy of either." That moment seemed to save me. I saw then that the only thing for me was to accept everything. Since then . . . I have been happier. It was of course my soul in its ultimate essence that I had reached. In many ways I had been its enemy, but I found it waiting for me as a friend. . . .
>
> Now I found hidden, somewhere away in my nature, something that tells me that nothing in the whole world is meaningless, and suffering least of all. That something hidden away in my nature, like a treasure in a field, is Humility. . . .
>
> It was the last thing in me and the best: the ultimate discovery at which I had arrived, the starting point for a fresh development. It has come to me right out of myself, so I know that it has come at the proper time. It could not have come before, not later. Had anyone told me of it, I would have rejected it. As I found it, I want to keep it. I must do so. It is the one thing that has in it the elements of life, of a new life, a Vita Nuova for me. Of all things it is the strangest; one cannot give it away and another may not give it to one. One cannot acquire it, except by surrendering everything that one has. It is only when one has lost all things, that one knows that one possesses it.

The first reading of Wilde's words were an "Aha" experience for me. Lights clicked on, and I suddenly better understood Jesus' act of footwashing. He, too, had lost about everything, everything except his integrity. He surrendered all he had and all he was to God. In giving all Jesus gained all, and he tried to teach this lesson to his disciples. He did so out of the deepest love for them. This fact may not be obvious at first glance but it is nonetheless true. One cannot serve another, in the deepest sense, unless the bond of love is between them. The footwashing was such a powerful proclamation of love the disciples recoiled at first. Carl Jung, the Swiss psychiatrist, helps us understand some of the dynamics at work in the footwashing.

> Love requires depth and loyalty of feelings; without them it is not love but mere caprice. True love will always commit itself and engage in lasting ties; it needs freedom only to effect its choice, not for its accomplishment. Every true and deep love is a sacrifice. The lover sacrifices all other possibilities. . . . If this sacrifice is not made, his illusions prevent the growth of any deep and responsible feelings, so that the very possibility of experiencing real love is denied him.[2]

Jesus was certainly aware of the fact that, as Jung pointed out, real love always commits itself, and he committed himself to the disciples.

*"He took a towel,"* a symbol of humble, obedient service and commitment. Albert Pine once said, "What we have done for ourselves alone dies with us. What we have done for others and the world remains and is immortal." Isn't he 100 percent correct? The greatest thing we can do is to invest our lives for others, and making an investment is always wiser than merely spending ourselves on ourselves. God takes our gifts, abilities, talents, and personalities; then puts them to work when we give them to him. You have a gift which only you can give. It is totally unique, as individual as your fingerprints. George Eliot put it this way:

God be praised

Antonio Stradivari has an eye

That winces at false work and loves the true . . .
And for my fame—when any master holds
'Twixt chin and hand a violin of mine,
He will be glad that Stradivari lived,
Made violins, and made them of the best . . .

I say not God Himself can make man's best
Without best men to help Him . . .
   'Tis God gives skill,
But not without men's hands: He could not make
Antonio Stradivari's violins
Without Antonio.

If Eliot's poem seems an overstatement, consider a different perspective given by Ralph Waldo Emerson's "Fable":

The mountain and the squirrel
Had a quarrel;
And the former called the latter "Little Prig."
Bern replied,
"You are doubtless very big;
But all sorts of things and weather
Must be taken in together
To make up a year
And a sphere.
And I think it's no disgrace
To occupy my place
If I'm not so large as you
You are not so small as I;
And not half so spry.
I'll not deny you make
A very pretty squirrel track;
Talents differ: all is well and wisely put;
If I cannot carry forests on my back.
Neither can you crack a nut."

Some of us seem to "carry forests on our backs" while others "crack nuts." The point is that both are necessary. Part of the symbolism behind the footwashing is bound up in the idea of service. I regularly meet people who honestly feel they have nothing to offer God. I try to probe a bit, and usually find one or more things they are good at and can contribute to the goal of the church. For example, our church recenty had a Christmas bazaar. Several men and women contributed handmade items and baked goods. Those people surprised the rest of us because they had told us that they couldn't do anything. The problem is that we define "service" too narrowly. Many feel they have nothing to offer in the realm of service because they fail to see that this is a broad category. God needed Antonio to make Stradivari's violins, and me to do certain things, and *you* to do other things.

King Louis IX of France annually washed the feet of beggars. This was supposedly an act which demonstrated his humility to the entire nation. It was that for Jesus, too, but more than merely a humble act. Submission to the washing was also a submission to Jesus' instructions to serve other people in a similar manner. This fact causes us trouble. We resist the idea of being servants. Yet, as Peter learned, without it we can have no part in Jesus' life.

My present church is small, but if every member took seriously his or her calling to serve, we would revolutionize our community. This failure to accept the call is a problem, not only in my church, but also in most other churches. Many members are "dead weight." A donkey and a horse lived together in their master's stable. The owner would load the donkey down with sacks of grain and lead him to market in town. The horse always went along but carried nothing. It pranced along and enjoyed the journey. One day the donkey said, "Look here, stop fooling around and help me carry some of this grain." "Forget it," replied the horse. "That sort of thing is beneath me." They walked along together for awhile, but the donkey finally collapsed and died under the load. The owner transferred the sacks of grain to the horse, and then flung the carcass of the donkey on top of that. The horse wobbled along and sighed, "If only I had carried my share of the load all along, I wouldn't be burdened with all this grain now, and dead weight besides!"

Jesus wants to wash our feet, but we don't want him to. We often prefer to keep him at arms' distance. But he does not force the truth of his love on us. He allows it to dawn on us as we become more used to the idea.

Jesus was not the proverbial "bull in a china shop" with peoples' emotions. He was more like the second stranger in the story, getting people to trust him, and then teaching them the truth. Jesus could have performed the washing before he did, but he knew the timing was wrong. The disciples still had much to learn.

Christ works with us today in the same way. He gains our confidence and trust before he gives us a towel of service. I personally find this exciting. The thought of the Lord caring how I feel endears me to him.

With the footwashing comes God's offer to forgive our sins. This is a daring and dynamic offer, one which we must renew each week. I recently saw guitarist Chet Atkins give a concert in Lexington, Kentucky. He started to play a certain melody but stopped to retune his instrument. As he was retuning he quipped to the audience, "I can't understand it. This thing was in tune when I bought it ten years ago." We all realized he was joking, for the thought of his expecting the guitar to be in tune after ten years was ridiculous. Yet Christians sometimes go on for years without taking time or effort to be "retuned" by God. Like old guitar strings, they rust, play off key, and finally break under the slightest strain. Jesus offered the symbolic forgiveness, but the disciples had to accept it. Peter was reluctant at first. He was a living example of a ditty I heard somewhere:

> Sitting still and wishing
> Makes no person great.
> The good Lord sends them fishing,
> But you must dig the bait.

Along with forgiveness, Jesus offers a task to do. One of the universal longings of the human heart is to accomplish something

significant and lasting. We admire presidents and famous design-
ers, for example, because they change things, and the result of
their labor goes on and on. Scientists estimate that the astronauts'
footprints on the moon will last one-half million years. This fact
boggles our minds because so few things we can do seem to last.
Yet, this is precisely what Jesus offers us—a chance to do
something great and lasting. Often our greatest contributions are
not even known to us. I can think of people in my past who have
made supreme contributions to my life, but I am sure they would be
surprised if I told them so.

We sometimes fear failure in serving God and other people. And
we should never take it lightly because service is no small matter.
But I agree with Edgar A. Guest's assessment:

> 'Tis better to have tried in vain,
>    Sincerely striving for a goal,
> Than to have lived upon the plain
>    An idle and timid soul.
>
> 'Tis better to have fought and spent
>    Your courage, missing all applause,
> Than to have lived in smug content
>    And never ventured for a cause.
>
> For he who tries and fails may be
>    The founder of a better day;
> Though never his the victory,
>    From him shall others learn the way.[3]

Yes, we will fail, and perhaps often. But the worst failure is not
even to try. Violin virtuoso Paganini told of the origin of the
Stradavari quartet. A wealthy patron of the arts purchased the four
valued instruments and gave them to top musicians. Whereas they
had been kept in "safe" storage, the patron said, "A silent
instrument, no matter how well made, is not fulfilling its maker's
intentions." The point establishes itself.

Jesus took a towel, the symbol of service. The facts show us that God calls—not the idle and lazy—but the busy, to be his servants. Consider the following examples from the Bible:

> Moses was busy with his flock at Horeb.
> Gideon was busy threshing wheat.
> Saul was busy searching for his father's lost animals.
> Elisha was busy plowing.
> Peter was busy fishing.
> James and John were busy mending nets.
> Matthew was busy collecting taxes.
> Mary and Elizabeth were busy with homemaking.
> Jesus was busy in his father's carpenter shop.[4]

Yes, the Lord expects us to be about his work. This is neither surprising nor a cause for despair. Charles Kingsley once wrote to a friend, "Thank God every morning when you get up that you have something to do that day which must be done, whether you like it or not. Being forced to work, and forced to do your best, will breed in you temperance and self-control, diligence and strength of will, cheerfulness and content, and a hundred virtues which the idle never know."

Having something to do motivates us and makes life seem balanced. Two of the most miserable months I have ever spent were when I was out of work. When I finally found a job, it was not glamorous, but I surely loved it all the same.

No "unemployment lines" exist in the kingdom of God. He expects us to seek places and channels of service, however modest they might be. As Ian Maclaren put it years ago, "The world cannot always understand one's profession of faith, but it can understand service." Jesus took a towel—will you?

# 6

# He Took a Cup and a Loaf

*1 Corinthians 11:23-28*

Pavlova, the grand ballerina, was once asked to interpret a dance she had performed. Her reply startled her questioner: "Do you think I would have *danced* it if I could have said it?" This reply makes us pause to reflect on the ballerina's meaning. Some things in life seem too packed with meaning, too shrouded in mystery, to be explained with frail words. A Scottish woman was asked to give an account of her religious faith. She said, "Weel, it can be felt but it cannot be telt!"

The answers of those two ladies give me a clue about what Jesus was doing when he took a cup and a loaf and shared them with his disciples. The act was symbolic: that is, it was an action which conveyed meaning better than words alone could. Jesus took two ordinary objects of his day, a cup and a loaf of bread, and showed his followers how much of God is in the ordinary things of life. As James White puts it, "Christ did not choose nectar and ambrosia, the food of gods, but bread and wine, the food of humans. Much of the sign value is lost when the bread becomes cardboard wafers, plastic fish food, or anything else than bread as it normally appears, tastes, and smells."[1]

Jesus took real stuff and made it into something special by consecrating it to God. This is why William Temple once called Christianity the most materialistic of all religions. He meant that God takes the things of this world seriously. After all, God created

56

them. At least a loaf of bread, a cup, and water are needed for the full expression of religious faith as Jesus knew it.

I recently heard a noted theologian admit that, at least for him, the celebration of the Lord's Supper in many modern churches is practically meaningless. I suspect that others feel the same way but do not admit it so readily. The purpose of this chapter, then, is to look at this symbol from a new perspective to see if we can recover its original meaning.

Dale Moody reminds us that for the first ten centuries the early church used bread which was a waffle baked between clay or stone bread prints, much as a modern waffle is baked between irons. Prints were carved or chiseled into the stones to make imprints on the bread. A lamb, a cross, or the letters AO (from "I am Alpha and Omega") would appear on the baked bread.[2] But why all the preparations to make a special product if the supper were nothing special? Obviously, this symbol as begun by Jesus and practiced in the early church had special significance to our spiritual ancestors.

Jesus called the broken bread and the poured-out wine a covenant between God and man. A covenant is an agreement between parties, but in the biblical sense, a covenant is more than a simple agreement. Robert D. Young explains it:

> The covenant theme goes back to Israel's dim beginnings, so that the more you know of those beginnings, the more lively your imagination becomes. "Covenant" recalls stories of the patriarchs, with specific scenes of Abraham's altar, Isaac's near-sacrifice, Jacob's dream ladder, Joseph's imprisonment in Egypt. "Covenant" speaks of the initiative of God that came when Abraham set out in faith, and when Israel was in Egypt's land, and when the people hung up their harps by the waters of Babylon and sat down to cry. "Covenant" recalls Sinai, the law to be followed, the law that blessed, and the law that was broken. It suggests acts of allegiance by families and nations. It operated when Joshua promised, "As for me and my house, we will serve the LORD." It also was behind those words of national significance, "If my people who are called by my name humble themselves, and pray and seek my face, and turn from their wicked ways, then I will hear from heaven, and will

forgive their sin and heal their land" (II Chron. 7:14). The covenant prompts allegiance by those under it. Then, too, other suggestions grow as Israel's history unfolds. Jeremiah and Ezekiel promise a new covenant. This time the covenant will not be an external one. It will be written not on stone, but in the viscera, written on the heart.[3]

Jesus, of course, knew that this was well within the consciousness of his original hearers. When he said, "This cup is a covenant in my blood," he hooked his hearers and brought their history to mind. But that effect was not limited to Jesus' first hearers. When you and I celebrate communion today, we are placing ourselves firmly in the paths our forefathers in the faith traveled. This is not a dead ritual, but a dynamic symbol, teeming with life and peopled with real humans like us. Fisher Humphreys says, "What really matters is that Christ is here joining the church in this meal. He is an unseen host sharing food for our spirits by giving his love, direction, and encouragement to us. There is nothing magical or superstitious about Christ's presence at the meal, but there is something profoundly spiritual and serious about it."[4] That is exactly it! There is something serious about the whole matter.

But what's in it for us? Why should we still observe this 2,000-year-old ritual? Let me give three reasons why I think Jesus used the cup and loaf as symbols of salvation, and what these symbols do for us today.

*1. Communion Heightens Our Sense of Perception.* Exactly four months ago from the time I first wrote these words, my wife Carla gave birth to our twin boys, Christopher and Ryan. We had gone through Lamaze training for childbirth and thought we were ready for anything. The projected date for their arrival came and went, and so did a dozen other days. But still no babies. When Carla was two weeks past due, her doctor put her into the hospital to induce labor. He tried for two days but had no success whatever. At the end of the second day the doctor came in and said, "We really don't have any other choice. We'll have to do a 'C' section." Both of us had tried to brace ourselves emotionally in case the babies would need to be taken surgically.

Because the doctor knew me well, and because I had been with Carla during her checkups for the last three months of gestation, the doctor said to me, "Do you want to scrub up and be in on this?" My answer was yes. At 5:29 PM on September 18, 1981, my son Ryan was surgically taken from Carla's abdomen. Exactly one minute later, Christopher came along. Each was over seven pounds and was extremely healthy.

Even after these four months have intervened, and after I have missed countless hours of sleep (a common occurrence with parents of twins!), I can still vividly recall every detail of that surgery. I can still recall the pounding in my chest as I felt my heart would burst through my sternum. The room was cold and I recall shivering, even though I had on a surgical gown. I can remember some of the conversations the doctors and nurses had. I can still feel the warm tears streaming down my cheeks, making my mask soggy. I remember the look on Ryan's face when the doctor held him up just seconds after taking him from the womb. All this I remember—and much more!

The point of sharing this incident is to explain that all of us possess tremendous powers of observation and perception. But for most of us these powers are ignored or abused. The pressures of the workaday world seem to smother our perceptions while we only try to get by. I am that way, too, but entering an operating room and watching my boys being born was so out of the ordinary that it stripped away the barnacles of boredom from my senses. I literally could see, hear, feel, taste, smell, and experience life as never before.

In the same way, communion, the celebration of the broken bread and the poured-out cup, helps us to perceive more than we ordinarily experience. The quietness of the service (or what *should* be quietness) raises our level of perception. It helps us see and hear and feel and taste and smell. Samuel Miller, imagining that the cup and loaf are before us, questions us about our senses.

> What do you "see" in the bread and wine? How much of life and death crowd into them? How deep into sin and darkness and shame do you see, and how high into mercy and compassion and faith? How much of this world's anguish and its black hate and its spite, how much of man's incredible trust and bright willingness to suffer and his invincible hope . . . ? Do you see the wild grain, the tilled soil, the dark of the roots, the wet of the rain, the blow of the wind, the threat of the storm, the feel of the grain in the hand, the white flour on the stone, the magic of fire, the making of bread, the gift of eternal benedictions, derived from countless agonies, the mark of God's sustaining grace? Do you see the fumbling mistakes, the burnt hands, the laughter of ridicule, the harsh pain of hostility, the dull ache of fear, the cold thrust of sudden death, the fears and fury, the joy and peace, the thinking and dreaming, the labor and loneliness?[5]

Perhaps you will recall a little poem by an unknown author:

> Back of the loaf is the snowy flour
> And back of the flour the mill
> And back of the mill is the wheat and the shower
> And the sun and the Father's will.

The elements of what we call the Lord's Supper help us see God in the process of living, and to see other persons who laid the foundation upon which we base our lives. It helps us remember that ultimately our daily bread comes, not from the bakery down the street, but from our Heavenly Father. Jesus' comment here, "I am the Bread of life," stands out as a beacon to dispel the darkness of anesthetized senses.

Someone once described art as "a calculated trap for meditation." This image speaks to me and reminds me that the cup and loaf likewise form a "calculated trap for meditation." When we see and hold the elements, we are forced to remember and to search and to behold. Artist René Huyghe wrote, "Art is that medium thanks to which the ineffable does not have to remain imprisoned to

he secret places of each individual's life. Poetry and art are based
on images; and images possess the power of penetration into the
individual soul and extracting from it and communicating to others
its secret treasures."[6] To change the wording slightly, communion is
that medium which helps to unleash the inexpressable.

Merely to talk about this in abstract terms is not satisfying. It
must be something like Walt Whitman once experienced when he
went to a lecture on astronomy—

> When I heard the learn'd astronomer,
> When the proofs, the figures, were ranged in columns before me,
> When I was shown the charts and diagrams, to add, divide, and
>     measure them,
> When I was sitting heard the astronomer when he lectured with much
>     applause in the lecture-room,
> How soon unaccountable I became tired and sick,
> Till rising and gliding out I wander'd off by myself,
> In the mystical moist night-air, and from time to time,
> Look'd up in perfect silence at the stars.[7]

Why hear a lecture on astronomy when you can see the stars?
Why speak in abstract terms about what the cup and the loaf are all
about when you can experience it for yourself? The next time you
are in a worship service in which the Lord's Supper is celebrated,
loose your imagination and really try to *celebrate*. Reflect on the
elements and remember that the contributions of many persons lay
behind the bread and juice. Recall that behind the efforts of those
people is God, who lets men plant and harvest and make bread and
juice.

*2. Communion Also Creates a Spirit of Worship.* Because communion does heighten our sense of perception, it puts us in the
mood for worship. Many sophisticated definitions for worship exist,
but I usually think of worship as the perception and response by
men and women to God. In other words, we become aware of God's
presence and then respond to that presence. Christians from

different traditions respond in different ways, but all worship is basically alike in the sense that the Lord wants to be worshiped and makes his presence known. His people can then express their acts of homage however they desire. The form of worship is much less important than the mood or the motivation behind the form.

This is why the cup and the loaf are such powerful symbols. In them Jesus is remembered as the Son of God who willingly allowed himself to be sacrificed for his people. He is the One whose blood poured out like wine from a decanter. How could anyone meditate on these symbols and not be moved to worship?

The answer to this last question is that many *do* see the symbols and fail to worship. I think this is true because they have not recognized the deeper significance of the act. Dr. Eric Rust has given serious thought to this matter.

He has developed six implications of the symbol for the Christian church. Do not be put off by this theological jargon. His meaning is very clear. First, the Lord's Supper is an Acted Gospel, that is, it proclaims the Lord's death in an active manner. Second, it involves a Living Presence: it is a reminder that God is present. Third, this symbol is a Thanksgiving, sometimes called the "eucharist," which means "to give thanks." Fourth, this is a symbol of Sacrifice, because we are called by this celebration to sacrifice as Jesus did. Fifth, it is a Fellowship Meal, because it is taken in a community setting within the church and is a symbol of unity. Sixth, the Lord's Supper is an Eschatological Feast, which means it actively points ahead to a time when Christ will feed his people in a new age. Jesus said in Mark 14:25, "Verily I say unto you, I will drink no more of the fruit of the vine, until that day that I drink it new in the kingdom of God."[8]

Yes, the cup and loaf are powerful symbols of *all* that Christ did for us and will do for us. It is understood and appreciated most clearly in worship, because it is in worship that we open ourselves to God.

Do you know anyone (perhaps yourself?) whose life seems, for want of a better word, empty? That this is a condition of many people today is no secret. Even many so-called middle-class people who have no lack of the basic necessities seem to feel useless and without purpose. Psychologist Rollo May expressed it:

> It may sound surprising when I say, on the basis of my own clinical practice as well as that of my psychological and psychiatric colleagues, that the chief problem of people . . . is 'emptiness.' By that I mean not only that many people do not know what they want; they often do not have any clear idea of what they feel. When they talk about lack of autonomy, or lament their inability to make decisions—difficulties which are present in all decades—it soon becomes evident that their underlying problem is that they have no definite experience of their own desires or wants. They feel swayed this way and that, with painful feelings of powerlessness, because they feel vacuous, empty. . . .[9]

I have felt this way and suspect that you have also. Personally, I find that one of the best cures for my problem is meaningful worship. I purposefully use the word "meaningful" because worship can be as empty as a bubble and useless. But it can be a joyous time of celebration, reflection, and fellowship. Worship, especially when the Supper is involved, is a time of spiritual fullness and wholeness. Lewis Rhodes reminds us that in such a case the breaking of bread is more than a symbol because persons interacting cannot be a *mere* symbol. He notes that the Supper bestows wholeness, not as "an objective means of grace, but a time, condition, attitude, action, and experience in which wholeness comes. Wholeness is not an absolute to be achieved and held; it is a condition like soundness and health. It is a quality of living, being, acting, becoming. Wholeness is not something one gets, but a way of living and relating."[10]

Rhodes has picked up on what seems to be an extremely important concept. Worshiping is not something we do in a vacuum nor is observing the Lord's Supper. If we do it in the right motivation and spirit, then we cannot but help feeling that we are part of something vital which is happening, namely, the meeting of God and other persons on a deep level. The masks are stripped away, and conventional "how are you's" are replaced by, "I experience you as a person of worth and as one whom I can trust." The latter may never be articulated, but is nevertheless expressed in attitudes and actions.

Many of you reading this book are laypersons. Suppose that you determine to make worship in general and communion in particular rich and meaningful. What do you think you, as a layperson, could do to create an atmosphere for growth, health, and mutual support? You might try to do this by telling your pastor that you have been thinking about the meaning of worship. Tell him that you have been in prayer about how worship proceeds and about what happens to people in the gathering. Suggest ways the worship period might be improved and made more meaningful and worthwhile.

And now a word to my fellow pastors. You and I have no monopoly on creativity. Any number of people in our churches are as creative, or more so, than we are. If they have ideas about worship and the observance of communion, give them a sympathetic hearing and seriously consider their ideas. Remember, you and I have to worship too, and a layperson's suggestions about possible improvements might be God's communication to us.

In an intriguing book, *Worship As Pastoral Care*, William H. Willimon suggests that healthy worship helps to produce healthy persons.

> Psychological study indicates that personalities change and mature most easily in a supportive environment that encourages them to experiment with new patterns of behavior. While the relatively safe, structured, patterned environment of corporate worship will undoubtedly attract some dependent persons who use the supportiveness of group worship for regression rather than growth, liturgy can provide a setting for risk and innovation within the personality-group and individual personalities. Public worship is always an invitation to the

individual to risk communion, to move out from oneself into the larger body; but it should be an invitation given within an environment where refusal to accept the invitation is always permissible and forced togetherness is avoided.[11]

I think he is correct. When one feels good about himself and his relationships with others and God, he naturally is a healthier and happier person. In this way, worship, and especially the celebration of the Lord's Supper, contributes to the overall health and well-being of the person worshiping.

3. *Communion Forges a Unity Among God's People.* Several years ago when the present Pope was elected to his position, a member of my church prayed for him one Sunday morning, asking God to bless him. A visitor said to me after worship that morning, "You know, I have never heard a Baptist pray for anyone who is not a Baptist. I think that was great!" I understood what the visitor was trying to say, but it was really an indictment against those of us who feel that we have God in our hip pockets, or that we have a privileged position. The plain fact is that we are members of the human race, and as such we have a religious duty to treat others as our brothers and sisters. Although the church has always taught this, it has not always practiced it.

Given the situation of global conflict and tension, it seems to me that we all need each other now more than ever. I am well aware of how easy it is to overlook those in need or those who are different from us. For example, as I was writing this paragraph, a lady knocked on my door to ask for emergency food assistance. I could have said, "Lady, I'm sorry but I'm writing a book. Besides, I'm facing a deadline!" But I took a little time to help her, because in the final analysis this lady who was down on her luck is my sister in Christ. I need her as much as she needs me.

An ironic fact is that the church, which should be the one place where all are welcomed and made to feel important, is often a cold, uncaring place where strangers are made to feel unwelcomed and unwanted. I wonder if this is why some people feel more comfortable going to a local bar than they do going to a local church. David Steele has a humorous—and poignant!—poem entitled, "David Danced—Michal Watched." This poem tells about David's struggle to express himself in worship by dancing, and about Michal's disgust with his gestures. Steele sees Michal putting David down in subtle, and not so subtle, ways, trying to make him refrain from making a public spectacle of himself. David finally gave in to the pressure and stops. The poem ends with these two stanzas.

> Churches these days
> Talk a lot about Praise
> And the Joy that accomp'nies the Good News.
> But don't tap your feet
> Or get out of the seat
> For Michal still lurks in the pews.
>
> And when you have ended
> She might be offended.
> And so it is better by far
> To act out your praise
> On those great joyful days
> With some friends at the neighborhood bar.[12]

No, I am not suggesting that you drop this book and make a mad dash for a bar. But I would like to see churches be a little more open and accepting. Is it not strange that we can help people deal with tragedies, but not with triumphs?

We need each other, both in joys and in failures. This is precisely what communion tells us. It is a powerful symbol of our kinship in Christ. William Hulme summed it up when he wrote:

> The Lord's Supper . . . is a healing antidote for guilt and estrangement; however, [it] has suffered from the distortions of an individualistic piety. . . . The trend was either toward the assurance of personal forgiveness and intimacy with God or toward the individual reception of sanctifying grace. These are no longer predominant emphases. In their stead is the corporate significance . . . It is not the

individual believer who receives from the Lord but the fellowship of believers, who receive also from each other.[13]

This reminds me of a custom the early church had, called "passing the peace." The Christians passed around the bread and held it for each other as they broke off a piece for communion. They blessed each other with words such as, "The Lord bless you and give you peace," when they passed the loaf on to another. They realized that in the deepest sense they were members one to another. They belonged and felt accepted.

The Lord's Supper thus has everything to do with the expression and formation of community. In our hunger for community, we should not forget that the central, historic, communal act for the church has been the celebration of the Lord's Supper. St. Augustine helped the church of his day recapture this emphasis. He wrote:

> The faithful acknowledge the body of Christ when they are not ashamed to be the body themselves. . . . That is why the apostles explain the meaning of this bread to us with the words: "We are many are one body, one body" (I Cor. 10:17). O Sacrament of love! O sign of unity! . . . Whoever seeks life can find a source of life here. Let him come forward and let himself be incorporated, and he will be given life. Let him not shrink back from the binding of the members to one another . . . Let him hold on firmly to the body.

This is exciting but, at least for me, very hard to remember. I seem pressured on every side by this person wanting this and that organization needing that. The irony is that I am around people so much that I tend to overlook them. By this I mean I get suspicious. Everyone seems to want something from me, so I keep my emotional distance at times. But the cup and loaf arise again and again in my consciousness. They present themselves to me as symbols of my brotherhood with all people, even the lady who wants me to solve all her problems, or that fellow who wants to dump fifty-five years of his anger on my back. Frederick Buechner expressed what I am trying to say:

To eat this particular meal together is to meet at the level of our most basic humanness, which involves our need not just for food but for each other. I need you to help fill my emptiness just as you need me to help fill yours. As for the emptiness that's still left over, we're in it together, or it in us. Maybe it's most of what makes us human and makes us brothers.

The next time you walk down the street, take a good look at every face you pass and in your mind say *Christ died for thee*. That girl. That slob. That phony. That crook. That saint. . . . *Christ* died for thee. Take and eat this in remembrance that Christ died for *thee*.[14]

Jesus took a cup and a loaf. He used them to sharpen the senses of perception of his followers. He created a spirit of worship with this symbol. And he forged a unity among all the peoples of the earth who call him Lord. Perhaps our prayer, then, ought to be the one which Ralph Sockman prayed:

Give us this day, O God, enough to live for as well as enough to live on, for we need faith great enough to give us purpose, and hope strong enough to give us heart, and love rich enough to give us comradeship.[15]

Can you say "amen" to this?

# 7

# He Took His Disciples

*Luke 18:31-34*

One of the earliest memories I carry with me of a church experience is a revival meeting I attended as a child. Many of the specific details have escaped me now, but I can still remember one particular night of the meeting.

The evangelist (whose name I don't even remember) talked about doubting Jesus. He thundered and threatened and spoke as if he had a corner on God. One of the things he did was to imply that if we, the members of the congregation, did not understand the mysteries of God, it was because we were sinful and not genuinely faithful. The preacher spoke on the way we could be absolutely certain of our faith.

Much of his message is no longer a part of my memory, but that part about being absolutely sure in all matters of faith is riveted to my memory. Even as a young boy that sort of thinking troubled me. It still does. To equate honest questioning and reverent doubt with sin is not only arrogant—it is silly. No one knows it all. No one understands the fullness of God, not even that evangelist.

When I was growing up in Evangeline, Louisiana, I worked on a rice farm for a while and in the oil fields at other times. I tried to take my religion seriously. For me, when I was toiling in a rice field or on a drilling rig, faith was not a matter to be debated, nor was it a question of absolutes. ("You can be *absolutely sure* about your religion.") Faith was simply what got me through some tough days and helped set the course for my life.

As I reflect back about that revival meeting, I am impressed with how wrong that preacher really was. First of all, people should not be made to feel guilty for not understanding all there is to know about Christianity. Further, not even Jesus' own disciples fully comprehended all that Jesus hoped to accomplish. Luke's account of Jesus' conversation with the twelve disciples speaks to me because I can so easily identify with them. Like them, I don't know what it all means. Like them, my puzzlement over the depths of Jesus' influence sometimes makes me feel left out.

But what happens to people who feel fuzzy in their faith like the disciples? Does their lack of understanding automatically condemn them to hell? Of course not! *All* Christians have much to learn. No one, not even pastors and seminary teachers, ever have it all put together.

Luke's account of our story about Jesus and the disciples shows us that sometimes even the most spiritual people overlook important issues of faith. A couple of issues surface here which ought to make us a little bit cautious in our faith.

*1. Expectations Sometimes Cloud Reality.* The disciples seemed to expect a political *coup d'etat.* Jesus, they felt, would wipe out the hated Romans with some sort of heavenly power and establish his kingdom on earth. Because they expected this to happen, they were bitterly disappointed when Jesus chose another course of action. Verse 34 of Luke 18 clearly indicates how much in the dark the disciples really were.

When I first entered college, I had firmly in mind what I expected that experience to be like. In reality it was vastly different. It was so different, in fact, that after three semesters I dropped out for a few months and then transferred to another school. My experience was not unique. Many of my friends did the same. Reality did not match expectations. Alan W. Watts, a thinker and author, made an interesting observation regarding what is real versus what we expect.

> One of the most common ways of trying to fix life into rigid definitions is to qualify something, whether a person, a thing, or an idea, with the statement, "This belongs to me." But because life is this elusive and perpetually changing process, every time we think we have really taken possession of something, the truth is that we have completely lost it. All that we possess is our own idea about the thing desired, an idea which tends to remain fixed, which does not grow as the thing grows.[1]

The disciples thought they had religion nailed down, but they found it to be a moving target. Jesus would not be squeezed into their mold, and his actions puzzled and confused his twelve obtuse followers. Mark Twain once noted, "Loyalty to a petrified opinion never yet broke a chain or freed a human soul."

Just because we might have specific ideas about religion, those ideas are not automatically right. They might simply be "petrified opinions." Christian disciples of the present era need ever to be on their toes for updating and refining their ideas about who God is and what faith means. Jesus' taking his disciples on a mini-retreat was a symbol of renewing those ideas.

That our expectations can get in the way of reality is, quite frankly, to be expected! Many of the early immigrants to the United States had certain opinions and views about what they would find here. Some found a country and a people decidedly different from what they expected. Some even returned to their original homelands because they were so bitterly disappointed. John Claypool declares that disillusionment comes from illusions. He means that a warped and distorted view of the way things really are may set us up for trouble.

We will do well to pay attention to what Wayne Oates calls the "Law of Realism." Suppose, he says, someone we are close to rejects us or tells us we are 100 percent no good. At first we might make excuses for that person, claiming he or she is merely upset.

But to adopt this form of excuse-making is to deny what may actually be happening. The other person may *really* reject us, and we may be powerless to do anything about it except make a clean break. As Oates puts it, "Only a clean break with our dreams and a frank acceptance of reality provides a realistic basis for discovery of a new way. Only then can our perception see a new design in the pieces, a new way through the tragedy, a new direction of creativity in the chaos."[2]

Look again at Jesus' disciples. Jesus was a mystery to them. What they expected to happen did not occur, and what they did not expect did happen. Isn't that like all of life? We think we have everything figured out, and then along comes something to shatter our dreams. A sharp pin of reality bursts our balloons of illusion. One might dream of becoming a successful businessman, for example, but end up at retirement having had only a mediocre career. Or one might want to get married and have a large family, but discover he is sterile and must remain childless. These, and countless other situations, seem at times to conspire against us. But a little realism goes a long way.

Hans Christian Andersen, the beloved storyteller, always carried a rope with him in his travels, in case of a fire. If he stayed in a hotel on the second story or higher, the rope would be his escape route from the window if fire ever broke out. That rope is now on display in the museum adjacent to Andersen's birthplace in Odense, Denmark. It is a good idea to be practical—to pack along a little rope, a touch of realism.

I have a friend who is not a Christian. He is serious in his unbelief because he will not talk about it flippantly. When he does open up about it, he explains that he does not believe in God because most of the people he knows who do believe are, in his term, "silly." He explained that these believers are the most unrealistic people he has encountered. The world is in a terrible mess with threats of nuclear annihilation, poverty, and pollution. But do these believers do anything positive about it? According to my friend, the Christians would rather gather in stained-glass bunkers and talk about how, when the world ends, they will be OK.

My friend has a valid point. If faith is nothing more than a life preserver on a listing ship, then it is selfish and therefore sinful. His wish that Christians be more realistic about the world is an important word for us Christians to heed.

In his book, *Brother to a Dragonfly*, Will Campbell tells about a friend of his likening the church to an Easter chicken. This man bought a chick which had been dyed deep purple and gave it to his daughter for Easter. At first she loved it, "But pretty soon that baby chicken started feathering out. You know, sprouting little pin feathers. Wings and tail and all that. And you know what? Them new feathers weren't purple. No sirree bob, that . . . chicken wasn't really purple at all. That . . . chicken was a Rhode Island Red. And when all them little red feathers started growing out from under that purple it was one (heck) of a sight. All of a sudden Karen couldn't stand the chicken anymore." This man took the chicken out to the chicken pen and turned it loose with the others. The result was, in his mind, a parable about the church.

"It was still different, you understand. That little chicken. And the other chickens knew it was different. And they resisted it. . . . Pecked it, chased it all over the yard. Wouldn't even let it get on the roost with them. And that little chicken knew it was different too. It didn't bother any of the others. Wouldn't fight back or anything. Just stayed by itself. Really suffered, too. But little by little, day by day, that chicken came around. Pretty soon, even before all the purple grew off it, while it was still just a little bit different, that . . . thing was behaving just about like the rest of them chickens. Man, it would fight back, peck . . . the ones littler than it was, knock them down to catch a bug if it got to it in time.

Yes siree bob, the chicken world turned that Easter chicken around. And now you can't tell one chicken from another. They're all just alike. The Easter chicken is just one more chicken."

Will Campbell said he told his friend that the chicken was still useful because it laid eggs. His friend shot right back,

"Yea, Preacher Will. It lays eggs. But they all lay eggs. Who needs an Easter chicken for that? And the Rotary Club serves coffee. And the 4-H Club says prayers. The Red Cross takes up offerings for hurricane victims. Mental Health does counseling, and the Boy Scouts have youth programs."[3] The implied question was clear: *What unique thing does the church do?*

This man was saying something which Christians need to hear. We must be realistic about our place and function in the world. Has God really transformed us or are we just "another chicken?" The church has always been guilty of doing foolish things. For example, one church in the Middle Ages instigated a policy known as the Truce of God. It forbade private warfare on Friday, Saturday, and Sunday. But why not forbid war altogether?

You and I live our lives based on what we perceive to be real. If that reality shifts, or at least our perception of that reality, then our whole lives change. Orlo Strunk, Jr., observes that we live by facts (reality) but also by metafacts—"those meanings and extra perceptions which take you and me beyond the ordinary facts of reality."[4] Strunk is a counselor and notes that much of his counseling involves the checking and rechecking of personal perceptions against the claims of reality.

For example, a person may feel unloved because he thinks he is unlovable. A counselor's job is to check out that perception to see if it is real. Strunk puts it like this: "I am personally convinced that one of the major factors preventing you and me from discovering the secret Self is that an encrustation of thoughts and beliefs, feelings and bodily needs, too often take possession of the central region. Many of life's experiences, including much of society's expectations and demands, lay upon the secret Self layer after layer of false ideas, negative feelings, and views of the body and its needs." By the "secret Self" he means who a person essentially and basically is. We must see that much of what we perceive as being real is simply the views and opinions which other people have laid on us.

Isn't that precisely what happened to Jesus' disciples? They were placing their expectations on what custom and tradition had led them to expect, rather than on what Jesus had told them. False expectations sometimes cloud reality. Jesus tries to cut through those false expectations and offer a new angle of vision.

In a most helpful book, *Listening As a Way of Becoming*, Earl Koile has pointed out that false expectations about what others say to us often blocks communication. Koile writes, "Listening and hearing in sensitive ways are open mine shafts to understanding and to an infinite variety of pleasing human relationships. Yet our potential for focused and sensitive listening often remains embedded within us, raw and unrefined, like a rich lode of unmined ore. Our views and understanding of one another also can become distorted when our listening gets cluttered and blocked by the prejudices we bring out of our past, and by the myriad of emotional barriers and biases in our day-to-day relationships."[5]

I can really identify with Koile's conclusion. I am often guilty of categorizing people and thinking I already know what they will say before they say it. For example, I know a lady whom I had pidgeon-holed as rather dull. But one day in conversation I was surprised by her sensitivity and comprehension of what was going on. I went home praying for forgiveness for having done to her exactly what I despise other people doing to me. Many are the times when I have walked into a room or a house and heard something like this: "Oh, oh, we can't cuss no more. He's the preacher!" "He's the preacher"—I *hate* being treated like a thing, or as merely a decoration. I want people to know me and to appreciate me for who I am. Everybody wants and deserves this same thing.

Jesus' disciples were guilty of the kind of narrowing of their opinions about their Master that I am describing. *We do not need to listen,* they thought. They already knew who he was and what he would do. But the surprise was on them! False expectations, regarding words or actions, can cloud reality.

Closely related to the fact of clouded expectations is this:

*2. Inability to Face Truth Blocks Noble Action.* Winston Churchill once said, "Truth is inconvertible. Panic may resent it; ignorance may deride it; malice may distort it, but there it is." "There it is" indeed! Although Jesus had told his followers what his intentions and purpose were, they just could not seem to get it straight. Their actions were based on false ideas, and they really did not know how to follow.

People sometimes arrogantly comment, "It doesn't matter what you believe, as long as you are sincere." But wasn't Hitler sincere? Of course it matters what we believe, because our actions are based on our beliefs. That is why Jesus' disciples had such a tough time after Jesus was crucified. They could not face the truth about what was happening. He had told them on two other occasions what would happen, but they could not buy it.

I have a friend whose husband left her after fifteen years of what seemed like a happy marriage. In conversation one day, she said softly, "I just can't believe it happened." Denial cannot change the truth, but sometimes it does work to soften the blow. Grief, for example, is actually our friend. It is nature's shock absorber. If, for example, we lose someone close to us, grief allows the truth of that loss to dawn slowly upon us instead of overwhelming us all at once.

Were the disciples experiencing what Erich Lindemann calls "anticipatory grief"?[6] This state is when a bereaved person goes through all the phases of grief in advance as a safeguard against the impact expected when the death notification occurs. Perhaps the disciples did know what was coming but they could not, or would not, face it. In either case, their actions betrayed their state of inner turmoil.

I empathize with them, too. I have had trouble facing the truth about some situations. As I reflect back over the situation with the Watergate scandal in our nation's recent history, I remember how many people simply denied that anything was wrong. The same thing happened regarding the war in Vietnam. Only now are some of the facts emerging from Southeast Asia concerning what Americans were involved in. It reminds me of the scene of three little monkeys, one with its hands over its ears, one with its hands over its eyes, and the third with its hands over its mouth. The caption reads, "Hear no evil, see no evil, speak no evil." But does that solve the problem?

Perhaps our trouble is deciding on what constitutes truth. Booker T. Washington tells in his autobiography, *Up from Slavery*, that after the Civil War many blacks realized that by being "called to preach" they could make an easy living. Washington remembered one itinerate preacher who would take a survey among his current audience to find a cause to champion. If, for example, most of the audience believed the world is flat, the preacher took the flatness of the world as his soapbox. The fact seems to be that most of us choose very carefully what we call truth.

John Roach Straton was a pastor in New York City during the first half of this century. He carried on a feud with the American Museum of Natural History in New York. In the Museum's Hall of the Age of Man was displayed the remains and restorations of fossil men. Straton charged the Museum with "mis-spending the taxpayers' money, and poisoning the minds of school children by false and bestial theories of evolution." He demanded that the Bible and representations of Moses be used to replace those "musty old bones." When lightning damaged one of the stone ornaments on the roof of the Museum, Straton boomed that this was a divine warning. But when lightning struck his own church soon afterward, he somehow failed to draw a similar conclusion. I wonder why.

Meister Eckhart, spiritual leader of another era, once asserted that neither all saints in heaven nor all the preaching friars and barefoot monks on earth could stand against one man moved by truth. This is a powerful comment, but I wonder if the reverse is also true—that one without truth can be moved anywhere by anyone.

In Ephesians 4 Paul wrote, " . . . we shall become mature people, reaching to the very height of Christ's full stature. Then we shall no longer be blown about by every shifting wind of the teaching of deceitful men, who lead others into error by the tricks they invent. Instead, by speaking the truth in a spirit of love, we must grow up in every way to Christ, who is the head."

The fragmentation of our knowledge sometimes gets in the way of noble action. Think of the technology available to solve the world's problems of hunger and disease. But what happens? Scientists often do not communicate with each other to pool their findings and solve real problems. Instead, they are hired by chemical manufacturing companies to patent and protect their findings, and work on such issues as split ends on hair and non-staining deodorants. Sure, those products are useful, but we could do without them, especially if people put their efforts into solving the big problems.

And are religious leaders any different? Religion in our world is as fragmented as the sciences are, and perhaps more so. Even within Christianity there are splits and divisions. One wonders why we cannot come together and work on some of the major concerns of our day. I am reminded of a statement by Julian Huxley: "No sensible man of science imagines for a moment that the scientific point of view is the only one. Art and literature, religion and humane studies are other ways of exploring and describing the world, and each yields results unobtainable by other methods."[7] If scientists, politicians, religious leaders, artists, and all who love people could simply agree on solving some of the major crises in our world, this planet would be a better place to live. But we can hardly agree on what the crises even are, much less on how to solve them. Some think our world's greatest problem is nuclear arms proliferation; others think it is pollution. Millions think it is poverty and hunger, while some feel it is spiritual depravity. The truth, it seems to me, is that *all* of these issues are major crises, and we must work to solve them. But first we must be willing to face the truth about ourselves and our world.

Part of that truth is that we Christians often fail to live up to the truth which our Lord taught us. I am reminded of a scholarly young man who ardently hoped to win the esteem of a certain young lady. But she was not overly impressed with him. To make matters worse, she never permitted the occasions of privacy he hoped for to advance his cause. One day while driving past a lake he saw another couple climbing into a sailboat. The girl, after seating herself gracefully in the stern, put a picnic basket at her feet. The man skillfully hoisted the sail. In a few minutes they were off, with a white sail against a blue sky. The heart of the scholarly young man watching this adventure leaped with excitement.

Having great confidence in the wisdom conveyed by books, he went to the library to study the art of sailing. He learned all that books and pictures could teach him, so he asked his lady friend to go sailing with him. She agreed, and off they went. He hoisted the sail with manly confidence and the boat moved out into open waters. But about that time a speedboat rushed by, causing a mighty wake. At the same time an unexpected gust of wind hit them. The long-hoped-for occasion of being alone with his love was lost, and the young man realized there is a vast difference between reading about sailing and actually sailing. His experience should remind us of people, including ourselves, who spend all their time reading, arguing, talking, wishing, and yearning about religion. We get nowhere because we do not relate our desire to action.

So what are we to do about it? First, we must acknowledge that we do not always clearly understand our faith. The disciples did not, the evangelist I wrote about at the beginning of this chapter did not, I do not, and neither do you. Realize also that we cannot always live in the perfect light of knowledge. We simply do not have all knowledge and insight at our disposal at this time. "Man's reach must exceed his grasp, or what's a heaven for?"

You and I find the truth by living the truth. In other words, do what you know to be right at the present time. As you do so, then more light will come, and more truth will be revealed. To quote Meister Eckhart again: "I have often said that a person who wishes to begin a good life should be like a man who draws a circle. Let him get the center in the right place and keep it so and the circumference will be good. In other words, let the man first learn to fix his heart on God and then his good deeds will have virtue; but if a man's heart is unsteady, even the great things he does will be of small advantage."

Jesus' goal for his disciples and for us is salvation, which is "wholeness, soundness, deliverance from everything that blights and warps human personality and prevents fellowship with God."[8] To achieve salvation of this sort takes time. This is why Reinhold Niebuhr wrote nearly a half century ago, "Nothing that is worth doing can be achieved in a lifetime; therefore, we must be saved by hope. Nothing which is true or beautiful or good makes complete sense in any immediate context of history; therefore we must be saved by faith. Nothing we do, however virtuous, can be accomplished alone. Therefore we are saved by love."[9]

We may not be able to explain the wind, but we can hoist a sail. We may not be able to explain everything about God, but we can lose ourselves in his service. A Chinese poet, Wu Ming Fu, expressed this thought:

> The seed that is to grow
>     must lose itself as seed;
> And they that creep
>     may graduate through
> chrysalis to wings.
>
> Wilt thou then, O mortal,
>     cling to husks which
> falsely seem to you
>     the self?[10]

"I am telling you the truth: a grain of wheat remains no more than a single grain unless it is dropped into the ground and dies. If it does die, then it produces many grains. Whoever loves his own life will lose it; whoever hates his own life in this world will keep it for life eternal. . . ." (John 12:24-25, TEV).

# 8

# He Took a Donkey

*Matthew 21:1-11*

Jesus took a donkey. A donkey? What was Jesus doing astride that funny little beast? Was that any way for the "King of the Jews" to travel? Would Napoleon have entered Paris on a pogo stick, or would George Patton have gone to Africa in a baby buggy?

The whole idea is almost laughable. It must have resembled a scene from a Barnum and Bailey circus. The animal sauntered into town while the "fans" lined the streets and cheered him on. On the donkey's back sat these people's new Messiah, so the people thought. They cut palm branches and laid them on the road for Jesus to travel over. Sir Walter Raleigh would have been proud.

The Jesus parade progressed on its journey into Jerusalem. The people shouted, "Hosanna to the son of David. Blessed is he who comes in the name of the Lord. Hosanna in the highest." Others stood by asking, "Who is this?" They were told, "This is the prophet Jesus from Nazareth of Galilee." Did this recognition mean that *finally* his hard work had paid off? Had the years of preaching and teaching taken affect in a positive manner? The fifth day of Jesus' arrival answered these questions once and for all.

Jesus and his coterie entered Jerusalem on schedule, but on whose schedule? The disciples'? No, because they had been trying to force his hand all along. They were like you and me when we pray, "O Lord, give me patience, and give it to me now!" Their schedule would have had Jesus throned and crowned by then, with them in places of leadership.

Was it Judas' schedule? No, because even Judas could not make Jesus betray his ideals. Was it *our* schedule? In a way it was, because Jesus entered Jerusalem for us.

But he did all this on a *donkey*, of all animals! It seems to me that animal was a powerful symbol of all that Jesus had taught and the life he chose to live. Let us explore what that symbolism was, and what difference it makes to us twenty centuries later.

1. *Jesus Identified Himself with the Old Testament Prophecies About the Messiah.* Zechariah 9:9 reads:

> Rejoice, rejoice, people of Zion!
> Shout for joy, you people of Jerusalem!
> Look, your king is coming to you!
> He comes triumphant and victorious,
> but humble and riding on a donkey—
> on a calf, the foal of a donkey. (TEV)

When Jesus decided to enter Jerusalem on a donkey, he intentionally accepted the interpretation of that event by the Jews in that city. Some would misunderstand, some would ignore, perhaps a few would realize what was happening, but more would simply be caught up in the excitement of the moment. Even so, Jesus chose to risk misunderstanding in order to show that what he was doing was not a gimmick or publicity stunt. He sincerely tried to tie his life and work in with his spiritual predecessors, the prophets of the Old Testament.

The entry created a crisis in Jerusalem. It was a time of decision for the people. They could either accept Jesus as the fulfillment of prophecy, or they could reject him, but they could not ignore his message. Jesus sent one of his disciples into the village of Bethphage to get a donkey. If anyone asked what he was doing, he was to answer, "The Master needs them," and he would be allowed to take the animal. Perhaps those words were some sort of code or password. At any rate, the words were understood to mean that God's prophet was in their midst.

Matthew 21:5 is sometimes interpreted to mean that Jesus rode two animals into Jerusalem:

> Tell the city of Zion,
> Look, your king is coming to you!
> He is humble and rides on a donkey
> and on a colt, the foal of a donkey. (TEV)

An early Christian painting shows Jesus astride a donkey with a colt walking beside them.[1] This procession was emulated in the Middle Ages on Palm Sunday processions. Sometimes a man on a donkey rode down the street, or a wooden carving of a man on an ass was mounted on wheels and trundled through the streets. Such a practice was called *Palmesel*, meaning "palm ass."[2] The Protestant Reformation of the sixteenth century ended this practice for the most part.

But what does all this tell you and me as inhabitants of a world far removed from first-century Palestine and sixteenth-century Europe? Albert McClellan, in his book, *The Hard Sayings of Jesus*, put his finger on an important point we would do well to consider. McClellan noted:

> Sending for the donkey was not a mere gesture. It was not an effort to hoodwink the people. No, there was nothing shyster about Jesus. He sent for the donkey because it was reality for him. He was not very God trying to be very man or very man pretending to be very God. He was truly both very God and very man. He sent for the donkey because his kingdom was different from all other kingdoms. It was not a kingdom of preference but of servanthood. He sent for the donkey because he was of the people, by the people, and for the people as much as he was of God, by God, and for God. He sent for the donkey because he was what he attempts to get all other men to be, manifestly himself.
>
> "Bring me a donkey." Most of us find we cannot live like this, and the reason too often is that we are not real. We are a bundle of irrevocable pretensions built up from childhood, and we are those to whom

appearances and seemings become securities. We hold all kinds of false ideas about how we should impress people—and everyone is surely trying to impress someone. Even the most extreme modern social cultists try to impress their peers, sometimes paradoxically, going "first class" by choosing "second class." For example, some of them wear faded and patched $ 25 blue jeans from the best store in town. How seeming can you get to be? Such people live not in the blazing clear light of the simple reality of God but in the light of their own selfish pretensions. If Jesus had not been of the people, by the people, and for the people, sending for the donkey would have been the boldest hypocrisy.

In Paul's language, the purpose is both to abase and abound, to know prosperity and poverty with equal grace, above everything else to be one's true self under God. What Jesus wants is no pretending. He wants bold reality. If it means to ride a donkey, ride a donkey. If it means to ride a golden chariot, then ride it; but above all, be authentic, be true, be real, be inwardly honest, and take your place as the servant of the people, for only the real authentic servants are truly "first class."[3]

Exactly! Christ wants his modern disciples to be "real," just as he was real. He followed in the steps of such men as Moses, Elijah, Amos, Hosea, Jeremiah, and Isaiah. They knew how to be true to God. Remember that Jesus was reared as a Jew. His Bible was the Old Testament. He bathed his mind in the Hebrew Scriptures and knew from the lives of the prophets that following God honestly and boldly is no easy task. Yet he chose this as a way of life, and his taking the lowly donkey proved it. His action in going to Jerusalem was so in tune with God's design for life that the stones would have praised Jesus' actions had the people failed to do so. Norman Nicholson's poem, "The Ride to Jerusalem," puts it into perspective:

The colt is tethered at the appointed gate,
The password known: 'The Lord hath need of him';
The trees are ready—this year Easter's late—
And willows wave their feather-fronds of palm.

The starlings practise on the chimney pots;
The thoroughfares of time are open wide;

Soon, now, the eyes shall weep for the blind streets,
The healing voice shall speak to the deaf road.

The window-sills are empty; no crowds wait;
Here at the pavement's edge I watch alone.
Master, like sunlight strike my slaty heart
And ask not acclamations from the stone.[4]

*2. When Jesus Took a Donkey, He Identified Himself with the Concerns of Common Men and Women.* Some people I know are put off by Jesus. They say things like, "He's just too good for me ever to know" or, "Jesus is the Son of God, so I can never really get to know him or be like him so I won't even try." What these people do not realize is that Christ *wants* desperately for men and women to come to him just as they are. The whole matter of the incarnation proves that God desires fellowship with people. In Jesus, God put himself in the shoes of humans.

Walt Whitman wrote about a fugitive slave hunted by a mounted posse with dogs.

The hounded slave that flags in the race, leans
    by the fence, blowing, cover'd with
    sweat,
The twinges that sting like needles his legs
    and neck, the murderous buckshot and
    the bullets—
All these I feel or am.
I am the hounded slave, I wince at the bite of
    the dogs;
Hell and despair are upon me, crack and again
    crack the marksmen;
I clutch the rails of the fence, my gore dribs,
    thinn'd with the ooze of my skin;
I fall on the weeds and stones,
The riders spur their unwilling horses, haul
    close,
Taunt my dizzy ears and beat me violently
    over the head with whip stocks.

Agonies are one of my changes of garments.
I do not ask the wounded person how he feels;
   I myself become the wounded person;
My hurts turn livid upon me as I lean on a
   cane and observe.[5]

Carefully note that second-to-last sentence: "I do not ask the wounded person how he feels; I myself become the wounded person." This is an apt description of the incarnation. Jesus became human *for* us—he became the "wounded person." As such, he identified with the hurts of people such as you and me. Remember, he took a donkey, not a charging stallion.

Jesus also identified himself with the tensions which other people face. When he came to John to be baptized, he was intentionally accepting his membership in a sinful society, even though he was without sin. I believe he was fully aware that the whole society in which he lived was sinful. Even so, he chose to identify himself with the people of his day. To me, that is one of the ways in which he powerfully said, "I love you."

In the television series, "All in the Family," Archie Bunker once said to his son-in-law, "Jesus Christ, Superstar! Your whole . . . generation—we try to talk sense to ya—we take you to church—we teach you religion—and you give us back the Son of God like he's some 'Englebum Hunkerdunk.'"[6] I admit that we sometimes try to make Jesus into the latest folk hero or rock star. But attempts to do so are not necessarily bad. We may try to do so precisely because we want so badly to believe that Jesus identifies himself with us. The message of the New Testament is that we need not transform Christ into the image of an accepting figure—*he already is one*!

When he took a donkey into Jerusalem he was saying, "Listen, my friends. I know how you are afraid and lonely and frustrated. I have come to liberate you from this. Only believe." And the people did believe, at least for awhile. But then they allowed themselves to

drift back into the same fetters as before, and only a few days later
the ones who shouted "Hosanna" shouted "Crucify him!" Their
lives became what Hermann Hagedorn describes:

> Lift up the curtain; for an hour lift up,
> The veil that holds you prisoners in this world
> Of coins and wires and motor-horns, this world
> Of figures and of men who trust in facts
> This pitiable, hypocritic world
> Where men with blinkered eyes and hobbled feet
> Grope down a narrow gorge and call it life.[7]

But Christ came to give abundant life. Why settle for "groping
down a narrow gorge and calling it life"? The gospel is that God
genuinely cares about our lives and has acted to free us for noble
action. Legion are those who care nothing for God or his action to
save them. Even God cannot carve rotten wood.

Theologians speak of what they call "inauthentic life." Many
people choose this. It is life with no reference to the saving power
of God in Christ. William Hordern describes it this way. "Inauthentic living means that one allows himself to be determined by the
world of things. Instead of deciding for himself he lets the crowd
decide for him. But even as he lives inauthentically man cannot
escape a sense that he is not fully at home in the world. He tries to
find his security in things but there is no final security there.
Because he knows that he did not bring himself into existence, he
knows that he cannot choose when he shall pass out of existence."[8]

Christ enables his followers to live authentic lives. This occurs
"when man takes responsibility for himself. He is liberated from
his past and open for his future. He is truly free. No longer is man
under the tyranny of things; no longer is he guided by what the
crowd expects of him. He dares to be himself."[9]

Only when we live as free persons in Christ can we expect to be
mature (which is what the New Testament means by the word
"perfect"). Unless we live this way, we are liable to fall for anything

(Eph. 4:14). Country singer Marty Robbins tells the story of Elvis Presley's famous manager, Colonel Tom Parker. When he was young and getting started in the promotion business, Parker once went into a small Southern city and rented billboards. On these he put just two words—"IT'S COMING!" Several weeks later he changed the ads to read—"IT'LL BE HERE DECEMBER 8. BUY YOUR TICKETS NOW." Many people purchased tickets and showed up at the town's community center on the stated night. Parker stepped onto stage to draw back the curtains which revealed a sign onstage, then got into his car and left town. The sign said, "IT'S GONE!"

This story is probably apocryphal, but it illustrates how easy it is for us to drift along with whatever everyone else is doing. Such drifting works well for cows, but not for people.

Jesus also identified himself with the freedom of common people. The German artist Bernard Plockhorst has a painting of Jesus' entry into Jerusalem on the donkey.[10] Plockhorst envisions children running before Jesus as they scatter petals from freshly picked flowers. Women lay before him hand-woven Oriental rugs, and men spread palm branches. The entire crowd joins in song and praise. While this is just an artist's version, I somehow think Plockhorst is correct in capturing the beauty and joy on the faces of those around Jesus on that day. This was humanity at its *best*— people acknowledging the Son of God. And Jesus accepted their recognition. The point is that all men and women are free to acknowledge Christ.

When God gave humans moral freedom, in some respects it was like giving a child a sharp knife. Some will hurt themselves, or others, with it, but some will put it to constructive use. That is what God wants us to do with our freedom—to use it constructively and creatively. God expects us to use our freedom of choice both to choose good and to choose to say "No" to evil. A European peasant was caught in the holocaust of the Nazi invasion. A Storm Trooper came to his cottage, dragged him out, and commanded: "From now on I am in charge. I will live in your house. You will feed me and polish my boots every day. I will be the master and you are the servant. If you disagree, I will kill you. Will you submit to me?" Without answering, the peasant gave over his cottage, fed the Nazi, and polished his boots every day. Months later the Allied armies came through the village and liberated the residents. They dragged the Storm Trooper out of the cottage. Just as they were about to take him off to a prison camp, the peasant went up to him. Standing proudly before the soldier, the peasant got right up in his face and yelled: "No!"[11] I am sure that Christ identifies with this kind of freedom which holds out for what is right.

   3. *When Jesus Took a Donkey, He Identified Himself with the Purposes of God.* "What in the world is God up to?" This is the question of countless persons. The best answer is to point them for clues to the life of Jesus as portrayed in the New Testament. God's purpose for fallen humanity is to redeem it. Jesus played a pivotal role in this purpose because it was through Jesus that God let us in on his plans. Jesus' ride into Jerusalem was a visual demonstration of God's love and concern for people. Henry Sloane Coffin put it this way: "The reported ride into the capital is so out of character that its historicity has been challenged. But if we have at all correctly sensed His mind, it is in keeping with His purpose. He is offering Himself publicly to the nation."[12]

   Rabbi Nahman of Bratislava, a teacher of another era, once said, "God chooses one man with a shout, another with a song, another with a whisper."[13] Jesus' ride into Jerusalem was a shout, a song, a whisper, and more. He gave himself to his people in the ultimate purposes of God. He wanted to be accepted, but he risked rejection. But it had to be that way. People must have the choice to say "No" as well as "Yes." But God comes again and again, in different ways, but always with the same message—"I love you." He speaks to us on a personal basis and never tires of leading us in his way. Remember, when God calls he never calls station to station, but person to person.

Henry Vaughn's poem, "The Triumphant Entry," stirs the imagination and lays hold of our willingness to submit to God's purposes for our lives. See if you do not agree.

> Come, drop your branches, strow the way,
>     Plants of the day!
> Whom sufferings make most green and gay.
> The King of grief, the man of sorrow
> Weeping still, like the wet morrow,
> Your shades and freshness come to borrow.
>
> Put on, put on your best array;
> Let the joyed road make holy-day,
> And flowers, that into fields do stray,
> Or secret groves, keep the high-way.
>
> Trees, flowers, and herbs; birds, beasts, and stones,
> That since man fell, expect with groans
> To see the Lamb, come, all at once,
> Lift up your heads and leave your moans!
>     For here comes he
>     Whose death will be
> Man's life, and your full liberty.
>
> Hark! How the children shrill and high
>     "Hosanna" cry;
> Their joys provoke the distant sky,
> Where thrones and seraphim reply;
> And their own angels shine and sing
>     In a bright ring;
>     Such young, sweet mirth
>     Makes heaven and earth
> Join in a joyful symphony.[14]

Jesus took a donkey. It still seems strange. But he knew what he was doing. George Buttrick once wrote, "He needed the lowly ass, the service of the unknown friend to whom the disciples were sent, and the friendship of his followers. He rode on an animal that was a symbol of quietness, not on a war horse; palm branches, not spears, were his welcome. When he died, a reed was his scepter. But he was kingly."[15]

The University of Louisville Cardinals won the NCAA basketball championship several years ago. They returned to Louisville on a jet, were ushered to a welcoming party in limousines, and generally were given the best of everything. Would it not have been a ludicrous sight had they come to town on tricycles, or on the back of a farm truck?

So Jesus took a donkey. He symbolized his identification with the prophets who came before him, with common people, and with the purposes of God. He rode *for* us. Let us accept his gesture.

# 9

# He Took a Whip

*John 2:13-22*

The human spirit naturally loves beauty. We seem to be drawn to it like bees to honey. Don't you enjoy standing with the wind blowing through your hair while watching the sun take its last breath of the day before it retires for the night? Don't you likewise feel your soul being fed while gazing upon some great work of art, such as a painting or sculpture?

Maybe it is because we do love beauty so much that this scene from the Gospels shocks us. Jesus took a whip and drove out the money changers. Isn't he the One whom the painters depict as having a halo, and whom they make look weak, if not anemic? Jesus and a whip—the scene shocks and disturbs us. It's not beautiful. It's not like Sunday School.

Don't despair. Explore the event and you'll see that beauty cannot hinder truth, nor can our concepts of what Jesus was supposed to do change what really happened.

*1. Jesus Took a Whip—it was his last defiance of an economic system which broke men's spirits, along with their bank accounts.*

It was a pretty good system, if you were on the right side of it. The conscientious Jews wanted to worship in tried and true ways. To do so they had to have animals worthy of sacrifice in the Temple. Not just any old sheep would do. It had to be the best. You can be sure they wanted to show off their sacrificial animals the way some of us like to show off new Easter clothes.

Now and again some oddball would raise his own animals for sacrifice. But most would buy it on the premises. No muss, no fuss. It's like stopping by the bait house before going to your favorite fishing hole, or going through the drive-through window at the burger stand. As Harold Bosley put it:

> So during the Passover the temple was like nothing else on earth. It was a thoroughfare, a stockyard, a slaughterhouse, a pen for fowls, and stalls for moneychangers with the men who ran each business pushing their own trade as hard as they could. The oriental bazaars of our own time come the closest to paralleling what must have been the situation in the temple on that fateful day when Jesus and his followers set about changing it. Whatever else it was, the temple was not a house of prayer, a place of worship![1]

But that's where the rub came. To buy the animals, the Jews had to have Roman coins. Some enterprising persons realized that if they set up shop in the Temple area, they could change the Jewish currency to Roman money and make a little profit, too. I changed dollars into British pounds a few years ago and lost money doing it. It can be a rough system.

It seemed harmless, really. So a few unscrupulous people made a few bucks. So what? What was the harm? Couldn't the people get by on a little less?

But that wasn't the real problem. The real problem was that the money-changing and the selling of the animals fostered a second-hand religion. When a man or woman raised a lamb, for example, they prided themselves in making sure that animal was the best, because they would be presenting it to God. But if you could simply buy one on the spot, it took nothing out of you. You could go through the motions without ever getting your heart right with God and other people. Jesus again and again counseled people to tend to the interior matters, and let the exterior matters fend for themselves.

Truthfully now, is a quick cheeseburger really as good as a hot, home-cooked meal? Is a religion that is all laid out for us on a silver platter by someone else really as good as genuine heartfelt obedience to the Spirit of God? We are experts on second-hand religion. We are sometimes so eager to believe what others tell us that we believe everything, and therefore believe nothing. We spin and turn like a weathervane in a storm, and end up pointing everywhere in general and nowhere in particular. "But all beliefs are equally good, as long as they are sincere," someone says. Adolf Hitler and Jim Jones were probably sincere.

So Jesus turned over the tables and upset the Temple treasury. The religious leaders would put up with his preaching, and even stomach his miracles. But his fooling around with the purse strings had to be squelched in a hurry. Second-hand religion has no patience with prophets who upset profits.

What the Temple scene was *supposed* to be like is depicted in Psalms. Consider the psalmist's counsel:

> How lovely is your dwelling place,
>   O Lord Almighty!
> My soul yearns, even faints
>   for the courts of the LORD;
> My heart and my flesh cry out for
>   the living God.
> Even the sparrow has found a home,
>   and the swallow a nest for herself,
>   where she may have her young—
> a place near your altar,
>   O LORD Almighty, my King and my
>     God.
> Blessed are those who dwell in your
>     house;
>   they are ever praising you.
> Blessed are those whose strength is in
>     you,
>   who have set their hearts on
>     pilgrimage. . . .

Better is one day in your courts
    than a thousand elsewhere;
I would rather be a doorkeeper in the
    house of my God
than dwell in the tents of the
    wicked.                                (84:1-5, 10, NIV)

2. *Jesus Took a Whip*—*a defiance of religious authority which made men less than men and God less than God.* Words are as slippery as eels. They confuse us and keep us mixed up. For example, we remind ourselves when some problem arises within us, "Aw, it's just human nature." "Just human nature"—as if that were a thing to be ashamed of, or a quirk on which we can blame all our faults. The problem is that this line of reasoning is just plain wrong.

Our humanity is not a stumblingblock. It is nothing to be ashamed of and nothing to be avoided at all cost. God made us human, and I think he knew what he was doing. We don't get into trouble when we're being truly human. It's when we are being *less* than human that we start having problems. Sin is not a result of being human, but a result of being *in*human.

The religious establishment of Jesus' day wanted to keep things under control. They had the formula for heaven, or at least they tried to convince the masses that they did. "Just follow the rules," they said. "Then everything will be okay." "Buy your sacrificial animals here. Exchange your money here." I'm sure it sounded like a carnival—"Hurry, hurry, step right up. See the fat lady and the two-headed donkey."

But the priests, at least some of them, had all the sincerity of a carnival barker. They convinced many that following the rules would lead to the Emerald City. But life, whether our everyday lives in general or our religious lives in particular, are not lived out of rules and regulations. They are lived out of personal relationships and trust.

For example, I try to take care of my wife, and I remain faithful
to her because of the personal relationship we have with each other,
and not because we have a document somewhere that states I must
do these things (even though we do have a marriage license). The
Old Testament prophets had told the Jews this very truth about
God. God was and is far less interested in all the religious hoopla of
the day than in how people treat each other and try to serve him.
Do you remember how the prophet Amos put it?

> I hate, I despise your feasts, and I take no delight in your solemn
> assemblies. Even though you offer me your burnt offerings and cereal
> offerings, I will not accept them, and the peace offerings of your fatted
> beasts I will not look upon. Take away from me the noise of your songs.
> To the melody of your harps I will not listen. But let justice roll down
> like waters, and righteousness like an everflowing stream     (5:21-24).

In the New Testament, James writes: "Religion that is pure and
undefiled before God and the Father is this: to visit orphans and
widows in their affliction, and to keep oneself unstained from the
world" (1:27). These are hard words—for their first hearers and for
us.

It's always easier to live by sight than by faith. So people build
about them a wall of rules and regulations which remove all the
mystery and ambiguity from life. And it works, at least for a while.
But life is not a package that can be wrapped up and tied with a
bow as if it were a birthday gift. Life is full of mystery, potential,
doubts, and faiths. Any statement of faith which claims to remove
the mystery and the freedom we have is not a true religion. It is a
fraud, masquerading in guise of God's authority.

Jesus faced this exact situation. The religion of his day made
men less than human because it lowered them to the ranks of
robots. "Observe this rule and follow this guideline and you'll be
OK. You don't need to think for yourself. We have all the answers."
Jesus said there was only one thing wrong with this approach—it
was a lie!

Not only did it lower persons, it lowered God. Instead of being a loving, active Creator and Father, it made God seem like a celestial slave driver. One slip up and, wham, you got clobbered. A well-known author once wrote that what he learned about God in Sunday School as a boy, instead of making him love God, made him hate God.

So Jesus lashed out against a belief which consigned men to the status of animals, and God to the rank of truant officer.

3. *Jesus Took a Whip—an act which virtually signed his own death warrant.* Rembrandt has a painting which depicts Jesus in the Temple driving out the moneychangers.[2] In the center of the picture one man's face is especially illuminated. His is the face of angered shock. But I think it's more. I think it is also a look of revenge. You can almost see the thoughts on his face: "I don't know who this country bumpkin is, but he'll pay for this. I guarantee it. He will pay!" I don't really know what Rembrandt had in mind when he painted that scene in 1626, but I suspect it was an act of worship.

The Gospels tell us that, after the cleansing of the Temple, the chief priests and the scribes sought to destroy Jesus. Incredible, isn't it? The priests and scribes were bitter enemies. Yet when faced with the possible loss of power, prestige, and money, they joined forces to kill Jesus. I suppose it was like the Russians and Americans joining forces to defeat Germany during the Second World War. Roland Bainton makes an intriguing comment about this situation.

> In the modern period, the episode of cleansing the temple has been adduced to prove that Christ would approve of taking part in war. Did he not display a fiery wrath? Did he not use a whip? Indeed yes, but a whip of chords is not an areuebus, a bayonet, or bomb. But I have seen no modern portrayals of Christ driving out the Kaiser, Hitler, Stalin, or Mao. Has secularism gone so far that an appeal to the example of Christ is not convincing?[3]

Some have wondered if Jesus understood what he was doing when he took a whip and drove out the moneychangers. Had he gone mad or was he possessed? Listen to the thoughts of Richard Watson Gilder as he explores this matter in his poem, "The Anger of Christ."

On the day that Christ ascended
    to Jerusalem,
Singing multitudes attended,
And the very heavens were rended
    With the shout of them.
Chanted they a sacred ditty,
    Every heart elate;
But he wept in brooding pity,
Then went in the holy city
    By the Golden Gate

In the temple, lo! what lightning
    Makes unseemly rout!
He in anger, sudden, frightening,
Drives with scorn and scourge the whitening
    Money-changers out.

By the way that Christ descended
    From Mount Olivet,
I, a lonely pilgrim, wended,
On the day his entry splendid
    Is remembered yet.

And I thought: If He, returning
    On this high festival,
Here should haste with love and yearning
Where would now his fearful, burning
    Anger flash and fall?

In the very house they builded
    To his saving name,
Mid their altars, gemmed and gilded,
Would his scourge and scorn be wielded,
    His fierce lightning flame.

Once again, O man of Wonder,
    Let thy voice be heard!

Speak as with a sound of thunder;
Drive the false thy roof from under;
    Teach thy priests thy word.[4]

Was he a gently mad Don Quixote, fighting windmills in a desperate attempt to win fame and the woman of his dreams? No, but he was anxious to see God's kingdom come in power and in deed.

4. *He Took a Whip*—*a gesture which shows there are some things in life worth taking an unpopular stand for.* Down through the centuries churchmen have tried to explain away the incident of the cleansing of the Temple. Yet all attempts at explaining away the incident are doomed to failure. Jesus was in fact angry. He was in fact outraged at the crass callousness of the animal sellers and the moneychangers. All the mental acrobatics in the world can't do away with that fact. Consider the ending of Edwina Stanton Babcock's poem, "Told in the Market Place."

'This temple is my house, the House of Prayer!'
    (His voice was like the wind that whips the leaves)
'But with your buying and your selling there
    Ye-Ye have made my house a den of thieves!'
Then little Rachael sobbed; 'Awful his mien;
His eyes are flames; I fear the Nazarene.'

But when the temple silenced—while a dove
    Fluttered and soared and beat against the roof,
We frightened beggars heard a voice of love
    Calling us gently; then his tender proof
He gave. He healed us! I, who had been
Blind from my birth—I *saw* the Nazarene![5]

This poem pictures a child being frightened by Jesus' wrath—"Awful his mien." But I think the description is accurate, and we need not explain it away.

Some things in this life *should* make us angry. Some things should make us want to get a whip and drive out the contemporary moneychangers. Doesn't the fact that little children aren't safe on the streets make you angry? Doesn't the fact that half of the people in this world starve while the rest of us stuff ourselves make you mad? Doesn't the fact that our government would spend billions of dollars for defense but only a fraction of that for real human need make you want to take a whip to the military-industrial complex?

A lady once told me that, as a Christian, she would never argue or fight with anybody about anything. The year was 1976 and we were getting ready to celebrate our nation's bicentennial. So I asked her if she liked being an American. "Yes," she replied. "God was in the founding of our country." I reminded her that we are who we are because our ancestors fought a bloody revolutionary war and snatched this land away from the British. She had no reply.

Jesus decided that some things in life were worth getting angry enough about to take action. A young communist once told missionary E. Stanley Jones that he, the communist, knew hundreds of fellow communists who believed in their way of life enough to die for it. Then he asked Jones, "How many Christians do you know who would do the same?" Jones admitted that he didn't know many. Fosdick once wrote, "All reformation is restoration." Jesus desperately tried to reform, and ultimately restore, the sanctity of the Temple. He knew that some things cannot be done without appropriate force, however much we might hate using force. Jesus did not offer us a blank check for anger or violence. He showed, however, that Christians are not wallflowers.

Jesus took a whip. He defied an economic system which hurt the poor. He defied religious authority which made men and women less than human and God less than God. He practically signed his own death warrant. And he showed that some things are worth fighting for.

The whip is a symbol of love in action. How will you use it?

# 10

# He Took a Cross

*Matthew 27:32-44, 1 Corinthians 15:12-19*

I bought a 35-MM camera not long ago and entered a photography class to learn how to use it. One of our assignments was to shoot several rolls of black-and-white film. The instructor cautioned, "Don't shoot just any and everything. Shoot only those things which capture your attention." With those words in mind I set out to buy the kind of film he had suggested.

As I walked up to the camera shop in Louisville, my attention was drawn to a strange sight. Workmen were busy razing the old Brown Hotel which once had been prestigious for its luxury accommodations. The hotel was about half-standing and half in ruins. Just beyond it stands the Cathedral of the Assumption. Its spire seemed to jut up from the wreckage of the Brown Hotel, and on that spire is a cross.

That scene struck me as a visual parable of the last two thousand years. Destruction and decay abound, but still the cross stands with its imagery of God's power intact.

I suppose if you were to ask 100 Christians what the central symbol of their faith is, most would answer, "The cross." But if you asked those same people to explain why a cross is that central symbol, most would be somewhat at a loss for words. I agree with Frank Stagg who wrote, "The death of Jesus (on a cross) is bigger than any definition, deeper and more profound than any rationale. Although man must seek to make it intelligible to himself and to others to whom he would proclaim it, all of its mystery will not yield to rational analysis."[1] Stagg is right. We cannot explain everything the cross means, but neither can we be content to move in the opposite direction. This chapter, then, is my attempt to look at the cross and answer the question, "What does it all mean?"

1. *The Cross Forms the Pivot of History.* Everyone knows that our very history is dated from the life of Jesus. The BC/AD division is an attempt by historians of former generations to comment on the importance of the life, death, and resurrection of Jesus of Nazareth. The cross is central in this history, forming a sort of hinge upon which all humanity has swung. The legacy of mankind is replete with the remains and effects of the cross. As George Willard Benson put it:

> Throughout all Christendom the cross appeared. It stood upon the altars of the churches, was carried in religious processions, and woven into the vestments of the priests, pictured on canvas and in stained glass, in frescos and mosaics fashioned with rich craftsmanship and hung upon the walls of cathedrals which were themselves built in the design of the cross. On every spire and many gables were crosses of iron and stone, and in the churchyards they marked the resting places of the dead. Everywhere were wayside shrines with crosses of wood and stone, Market Crosses of sculptured marble and Sanctuary Crosses to which men fled for refuge.
>
> The Crusader's sword was cross-hilted and every Knight dedicated his sword upon the alter and wore a cross upon his breast, as we went forth upon a crusade.
>
> The escutcheons of most ancient families bore it in varied forms and appeared frequently on the coins and medals of the realm. The crowns of kings and nobles were almost invariably surmounted by a cross.
>
> The prevailing use and influence of this supreme symbol of Christianity is remarkable. The study of its origin, history, and symbolism is an investigation full of value and interest.
>
> The cross is a symbol more universal in its use and more important in its significance than any other in the world.[2]

The cross was used at various times in history as an object of almost magical power. For example, relics of crosses were seen as potent protectors during times of war. During the siege of Rome by the Lombards in 756 AD, a procession of supplication was held in which a relic of a cross was carried around the city with the treaty which the Lombards had violated fixed to it. At another time, when the emperor Mauritius made his expedition to Thrace in 593 AD, the Byzantine army set out led by a golden lance in which was set a piece of the cross. Heraclius took a relic of a cross with him when he set out on a military expedition against Persia in 622 AD. Pope Nicholas I took with him a relic of a cross when he went out to confront the troops of Louis II in 864 AD. And Charlemagne used to carry with him a box containing a fragment of a cross when he went into war. All of these were alleged to be true "pieces of the cross."[3]

Other examples abound about how people have used the cross. An eighth-century English monk, known as "the Venerable Bede," attributed St. Oswald's victory over Welsh invaders at Hexham to the wooden cross around which Oswald and his Northumbrians made their stand. Bede told of the rough, wooden cross put together in the utmost haste and of Oswald holding it up with both hands as his soldiers heaped dirt around it so it would stand upright. When dawn broke, the invaders attacked, but were broken in vain against the rock of that cross which, as Bede put it, was "towering o'er the wrecks of time." Oswald's prayer was answered, and the invaders were repelled by the defenders of faith. Thus, a rough, wooden cross so hastily set up supposedly decided the fate of Britain.[4]

History pivots around a stationary stake known as the cross. Men and kingdoms rise and fall, but the cross remains. Gerald O'Collins says, "The crucified Christ forms a kind of axis of the universe. He hangs impaled between heaven and earth, his body stretched out in four directions and his arms open to the world."[5]

So we find that this cross has a magnetism about it, drawing both our attention and our obedience as Christ waits "with his arms open to the world." History moves away from the event of the cross, the crucifixion of AD 33, but it also moves to the cross, the meaning of an act of divine love in which God said "Yes" to the world. One Friday afternoon in Palestine a couple of thousand years ago there was an ugly sight and sound. As Wayne Ward wrote:

> All heaven and earth converge upon that central cross. The drama of redemption reached its amazing climax when human sin rose up and divine love reached down to that cross on Calvary! No words could possibly catch the despair which overwhelmed the disciples as they took the body down from the cross and laid it in Joseph's tomb. The drama was over. The King had come, but he was a King that nobody wanted. With wicked hands men had brutally tortured him, and his dead body was already in the grave, from which no traveller ever returned.[6]

But one traveller did return! Because Jesus took a cross and triumphed over it, all history is different. I am changed and you are, too. The crucifixion was a grisly deed, but it afforded God the opportunity to share his love with all men who will receive it.

A modern tragedy is that not all will receive that love. Some actively fight against it, but most simply ignore it. G. A. Studdert-Kennedy has a poem in which Jesus went to Birmingham, England. What happened?

> When Jesus came to Golgotha they hanged Him on
>     a tree,
> They drove great nails through hands and feet, and
>     made a Calvary;
> They crowned Him with a crown of thorns, red were
>     His wounds and deep,
> For those were crude and cruel days, and human
>     flesh was cheap.
>
> When Jesus came to Birmingham, they simply passed
>     Him by,
> They never hurt a hair of Him, they only let Him die;

> For men had grown more tender, and they would
>   not give Him pain,
> They only just passed down the street, and left Him
>   in the rain.
>
> Still Jesus cried, 'Forgive them, for they know not
>   what they do,'
> And still it rained the winter rain that drenched Him
>   through and through;
> The crowds went home and left the streets without
>   a soul to see,
> And Jesus crouched against a wall and cried for
>   Calvary.[7]

And if Jesus came to your city or county—would he likewise be ignored by "gentler" but more aloof men and women? The question need not detain us long. The fact is that he did come once and was anything but ignored. The rough-hewn planks upon which he died did not rot away with time. They formed a symbol in the religious consciousness of all who followed after Him that is now the zenith of all symbols. History itself has acknowledged this to be true.

2. *The Cross "Tips God's Hand."* Hebrews 1:1-2 reads, "Long ago God spoke to our fathers in many different ways by the prophets, but in these last days He has spoken to us by His Son, whom He made heir of everything by whom He made the world."[8] God had tried all along to tell mankind what he desired and demanded. His messengers were the prophets and patriarchs, people such as Moses, Isaiah, Jeremiah, Hosea, Joel, Amos, and others. But their words were misunderstood and their actions were ignored.

God could have given up in despair, but instead he chose to send his message of love through his Son. Jesus came following in the line of the prophets who preceeded him, but his was different. He was not merely a messenger—he was the *message* itself. He proclaimed, "If you want to see God, then look at my life." But you and I know what happened. People distorted his message and maligned his motives. His relationship to God was called into question so he was tried for blasphemy and executed like a common criminal. But a strange thing happened. The messanger who was also the message could not be squelched. His cross was therefore not simply a place of dying. It became a sign of life, a quality of life which cannot be bound by nails nor squashed by jeers. The cross thus became a symbol which showed what God had in mind all along. He does not like blood and gore, but God is insistent that *nothing* should stand in the way of his telling his people, "I love you, no matter what you do to me."

Second Corinthians 5:18-19 in Beck's translation reads, "But God has done it all. When we were His enemies, through Christ He made us His friends and gave us the work of making friends of enemies. In Christ, God was getting rid of the enmity between Himself and the people of the world by not counting their sins against them, and He has put into our hands the message how God and men are made friends again." The cross is God's instrument in declaring a cease-fire between himself and us. That is why I say the cross tips God's hand—it lets us in on what he is up to.

George Buttrick once wrote, "The magnetism of the Cross so strangely persists as to indicate a miracle. For why should anyone today trouble himself about a Peasant hung in an obscure land many centuries gone?"[9] This is a question which must be answered. Why bother about the peasant? Isn't that ancient history? I cannot believe it is. Atheism is the most intellectually lazy of all belief systems, because with just the wave of the hand or the shrug of a shoulder it claims to do away with all the difficult issues of life and death. But I do not believe these matters can be shooed away like one chases off a mosquito. They must be faced, questioned, and examined from every angle.

The cross, too, must be examined and reexamined to see what it reveals to us about God. If we study it long enough, perhaps answers will emerge for us as they did for a pastor who attended a community goodwill banquet. A fellow seated next to him wanted preachers to speak less about the cross so they would not stir up anti-Semitism. The preacher replied, "I am afraid you do not understand what the Cross means and does. It has inspired more sacrificial living and has transformed more selfishness than any other fact in history. From it flows the goodwill we desire in this town. The question is not, 'Who put Jesus to death?' but rather, 'What does his death mean?'"[10]

This fellow was on the right track. We must know what the death of Christ, and its symbol, the cross, mean to modern people. Harold Cooke Phillips gave the following advice to would-be communicators of the Christian faith: "Theology may soar aloft like an airplane into the blue yonder, but remember that the plane takes off from the earth, and against the wind. Remember too that it stays aloft and is guided in its flight by its contact with earth. Neither a theology that is other-worldy, nor a morality that is earthbound is adequate."[11] What we need, then, is not just idle speculation. There is enough of that already. You may recall that theology in the Middle Ages was characterized by the image of men sitting around the fireplace speculating on how many angels could sit on the head of a pin. As Harold Brierley reminds us, "The cross was not an afterthought, a theological device, for the redemption of a world gone wrong, but the 'Sign'—at once of a divine principle and its supreme historic manifestation, at Calvary—by which God is ever lifting this sad, errant and struggling world out of nature's darkness into His marvelous light."[12]

The cross is therefore the supreme symbol which tells us what God is doing in our lives—"lifting this sad, errant and struggling world out of nature's darkness." I do not see the cross as a dispensable means of God's dealing with us. If the cross could be tossed out, then so could our salvation. One theologian observed:

> Christian theology must be theology of the cross, if it is to be
> identified as Christian theology through Christ. But the theology of the

cross is a critical and liberating theory of God and man. Christian life is
a form of practice which consists in following the crucified Christ, and
it changes both man himself and the circumstances in which he lives.
To this extent, a theology of the cross is a practical theory. [13]

## Another thinker states the issue as follows:

Ecclesiologies that attend to the ministry, the resurrection, Pentecost
and the early decades of the Church's history—while studiously
ignoring the passion and death of Jesus—risk setting up false or
inadequate scales of success and find themselves wanting. By all means
let us ask how the gifts of the Holy Spirit should be freely and
responsibly used to build up the common life of the Church. Let us
reflect too on whether the Church faithfully journeys towards that
coming kingdom to which Jesus repeatedly bore witness in his ministry.
But we should also recall themes like suffering, failure, powerlessness
and abandonment. A Church born from the side of the crucified Christ
will bear in its body the marks of crucifixion. It is at our peril that we
fail to ponder and include in our ecclesiologies that profound "weak-
ness" which we see in the crucified Christ (II Cor. 13:4). [14]

In the cross of Jesus, God tipped his hand and let us in on what
he was doing. We cannot ignore that cross because to do so is to
tangle the lines of communication between God and ourselves.

3. *The Cross Demonstrates God's Identification with Our Struggles.* W. L. Stidger told of an experience he had one night in France
during the First World War. The first time he drove his supply truck
down the Toul road he was scared. The shellfire that peppered the
road was not his main fear. He was simply scared of making a
wrong turn with his load of supplies intended for the men on the
front line and ending up driving straight into the German lines. He
said he had a map, but admitted that map reading was never his
strong point.

After driving down the road for ten miles without headlights,
Stidger came to a crossroad. One road would carry him to his
destination, but the other would take him into "No Man's Land" and
into the German lines. He pondered which road to take. As he

stopped the truck he saw gleaming through the darkness the shadow of a cross. He went over to it with a shaded flashlight, hoping to find under the crucifix a sign telling him which road to take. He flashed his light on the cross and saw a skillfully carved body of Christ. Then his light fell on the writing above it. The words were, "Traveler, hast thou ever seen so great a grief as Mine?"

Stidger said, "Never did a single sentence carve itself so deeply and vividly on my mind as that one. Off in the distance I could hear the roar of the big guns. But there was a new peace and confidence in my heart as I climbed back into my truck and delivered my load of supplies. To this day, whenever I think of the loneliness, suffering and heartbreak . . . I remember that night on the Toul road and the sentence carved above that French crucifix."[15]

Often when I conduct a funeral service I remind the congregation that even in their pain and grief, God knows how they feel— He lost a son once, too. That thought often brings about relief from the loneliness some people feel. This is not merely a cute preacher gimmick. I believe it is profound theology. God, in Christ, experienced our world and all that it had to offer. The cross was not a decoy or a farce. It was real nails which fastened a real body to the beams, and real blood which dripped down to God's earth. And when Jesus died, God felt the pain. Why else would the sky have gotten dark at midday? In the cross God identified with our hurts and our struggles. The poet wrote:

> All living creatures' pain,
> The suffering of the lowliest thing that creeps
> Or flies a moment 'ere it sinks and sleeps
> Are too Redemption's tears and not in vain—
> For nothing idly weeps.
> Earth is through these fulfilling that it must
> As in Christ's own eternal Passion Chain,
> And flowering from the dust.[16]

It is true—"nothing idly weeps." Somehow in the grand scheme

of things, it all matters. I am but one four-billionth of the humans
living on the earth at this moment. That percentage is so small as to
numb the imagination. Yet I believe that what happens to me, to
you, and to all other persons, matters deeply to God. If I did not
believe this, then prayer would be ruled out and any sense of a
personal relationship with God is an illusion. But since God does
care and does hear me when I pray, I can likewise believe that in
the cross God has increased our mutual understanding.

Some people feel that the crucifixion was a hoax—that Jesus had
it all rigged and that he did not really suffer. "After all," they ask,
"if he really were God, then how could he have suffered? Does God
have feelings?" My answer is, "Yes, God does have feelings. His
heart broke when his Son died on a cross."

Jesus died but then lived again. In that living he took on a new
mode of existence which continues today. That quality of life could
come only through suffering love. An anonymous poet penned in
the poem, "Hope":

> He died!
> And with him perished all that men hold dear;
> Hope lay beside him in the sepulchre,
> Love grew corpse cold, and all things beautiful
> beside
> Died when he died.
>
> He rose!
> And with him hope arose, and life and light.
> Men said, 'not Christ but Death died yesternight.'
> And joy and truth and all things virtuous
> Rose when he rose.[17]

Hope cannot be smothered in a grave, nor can love be stifled
upon a cross. Christ lives today because the life he chose to lead
two millenia ago is a testimony to love. When he said, "Consider
the lilies of the field, how they grow; they toil not, neither do they
spin—yet Solomon in all his glory was not arrayed like one of

these," he was speaking symbolically of man's spiritual life. Someone has noted that, "The roots of the lily are in the earth. Its beauty and fragrance are the outgrowth of God's beneficent sunshine. The Cross planted in shame and ignominy has grown through the ages in the hearts of men to become the symbol in mystic beauty and power of the spirit of Jesus Christ."[18] This I believe is true.

Harold Cooke Phillips helped me personally understand a little better what the cross and God's identification with us are all about. Consider his counsel.

> As the late and beloved Hal Luccock has written, "Jesus was not crucified for saying 'Consider the lilies of the field how they grow,' but 'consider the thieves in the temple how they steal.'" It is evident that he aroused the bitter hostility and determined opposition of the social, economic, political and religious powers of his age. An irrelevant gospel would never have done that. And he predicted that his followers would be brought before governors and kings for his sake (Matthew 10:18), as they were and have been. But only a word that touched life deeply and widely and could have evoked such relentless opposition. The cross, then, is a symbol of the involvement of our faith in all that most deeply affects life. Sir George McLeod of Iona puts it vividly: "I simply argue that the cross be raised again at the center of the market place, as well as on the steeple of the church. I am recovering the claim that Jesus was not crucified in a cathedral between two candles, but on a cross between two thieves; on the town's garbage heap, at the crossroads so cosmopolitan that they had to write his title in Hebrew and in Latin and in Greek, at the kind of place where cynics talk smut and thieves curse and soldiers gamble . . . That is where he died and that is what he died about."[19]

In dying he lived. In giving all he gained all. In accepting the full fury of abhorrent hatred he let loose the most profound expression of love the world has ever known. In it all and through it all Jesus came to know firsthand what you and I face in the mystery we call life. He identified with us, and bids us even now to follow the path he has established for the living of our faith. The cross was the means to this end.

4. *The Cross Gives Us Power to Change.* Even if the cross did all the things I mentioned above, but did not enable us to change and become more like Christ, it would have been merely a futile mission on God's part. Without some power to back up its purpose, the cross would merely have been a gibbet with no far-reaching significance. But many people see it exactly that way. A novelist envisioned people in a little village going about the perfunctory business of observing Easter. "That way the Rosetrees spent their Easter, while for other . . . families, Jesus Christ was taken down, and put away, and resurrected, with customary efficiency and varying taste. Outside the churches everyone was smiling to find they had finished with it; they had done their duty, and might continue on their unimpeded way."[20] But is the cross merely a "duty" to be done so people can go on "their unimpeded way"? Is there no more to it than custom and convention, like the tip of a hat, or a prescribed table manner? If so, then all the followers of Christ have been guilty of pandering a gentle joker who imagined himself a king and the Son of God.

Whatever else the cross is, it is a symbol of the power of God which changes you and me if we allow it to. It does not simply cancel sin—it transfigures sin-distorted character so that the very memory of sins and their consequences become factors in the new life. When Jesus died, it was for a purpose and reason. An anonymous poet framed this idea in these words:

Under an Eastern sky,
Amid a rabble cry,
A man went forth to die
    For me!
Thorn-crowned His blessed head,
Blood-stained His every tread,
Cross-laden on He sped,
    For me!

Pierced through His hands and feet,
Three hours o'er Him did beat
Fierce rays of noontide heat,
    For me!

Thus wert Thou made all mine.
Lord make me wholly thine,
Give grace and strength divine
    To me!

In thought and word and deed,
Thy will to do; oh! lead my feet
Even though they bleed
    To Thee.[21]

Yes, the death was, as the poet said, "for me." It did something in my life. But how does it do so? What is there about my taking seriously the cross of a Galilean prophet? Charles and Marjorie McCoy have answered this question:

> How does the work of the transforming Cross occur in our lives? How can we so dwell in our faith that we are unable to break out from our old ways into new awareness and new action? By not letting our hearts become hardened against change, by desiring transformation, by imagining ourselves living the abundant life proclaimed in the Gospels. This means listening to Jesus and to the entire Christian story, not just with our ears to get the story accurately, not just with our minds to understand it intellectually, but listening with our whole selves, with heart and soul and mind and strength, until we hear in this story the story of our own life.[22]

The story of Jesus and his cross is really the story of every person in the sense of offering us a dynamic model of how life *can* be lived. His life was an absolute "yes" to God, even if it included a cross. This is not to say that God wills pain and suffering, but that evil men cannot thwart God's plans to redeem mankind.

Not long ago I received in the mail a tiny metal cross and a card with a poem on it entitled, "A Cross in My Pocket." The little poem tells about how we should carry the cross in order to remind ourselves that we are Christians. But if I need some external reminder or prompter, I might not be much of a Christian!

A modern theologian commented that contemporary Christians have taken the rough cross of Christ and smoothed all the splintered edges off, washed away the blood, and covered it with roses. Now, says the theologian, we see the cross as simply a tame piece of jewelry like any other, with little power to transform our wills or effect our lives. Is he right?

I recently heard Malcolm Muggeridge of Britain, a Christian intellectual, being interviewed by William F. Buckley, Jr. Buckley mentioned that talking about one's personal faith at social gatherings, such as a party, is a way to stifle conversation and make people feel uncomfortable. Muggeridge thoroughly disagreed, saying that people are hungry to speak about matters of faith and to know if God really does exist and if he can help people. This interview was interesting because Muggeridge moves in fairly high-class circles, and he realizes that even the rich and powerful need to know if the universe is friendly. Don't we all?

The bottom line of all religious thinking is this: Can God do anything for me, and if so, how? I believe the cross is the answer to this question. A story might help to illustrate how God deals with us. A child is lost in a heavy snow. He is unable to make his way home. His father goes to find him and bring him home. Several alternatives could be considered. The father could set an example, asking the child to make his way home by imitating the father, each making his path through the snow. But an example is not enough, because the snow is too deep for the child. The second alternative is for the boy to remain where he is and to have the father go home for the boy. But that would leave the child in the snow. A third way would be for the father to take the child by the hand and lead him home, breaking through the snow for the child. This way the boy finally gets home, but as one rescued. He walks in the strength of another.[23] This, I believe, is an analogy of what God did with a cross.

I had the opportunity to spend July of 1979 in Oxford, England, studying at Mansfield College. A street in downtown Oxford has a small black cross imbedded in the pavement. A sign nearby tells what it means. In 1555 two British reformers were burned at the stake on the spot where the cross now sits. These reformers, Hugh Latimer and Nicholas Ridley, tried to renew the church of their day, and met death for their efforts. Tradition says that as the fires were lit Latimer cried out, "Be of good comfort, Master Ridley, and play the man. We shall this day light such a candle by God's grace in England as I trust shall never be put out." Latimer was right. His death inspired other people to take up his work and see it through. As I stood on that Oxford street and pondered what happened, I could not help thinking about another person who died for his beliefs. He, too, lit a candle which can never be extinguished. He, too, gave his life so that others might live, but this one was nailed to a cross, cursed and spat upon, and stripped naked. When this man died, the world began to learn how to live. The cross gives its power to any who will accept it:

> See there! God's signpost, standing at the ways
> Which every man of his free will must go—
> Up the steep hill, or down the winding ways,
> One or the other, every man must go.
>
> He forces no man, each must choose his way,
> And as he chooses, so the end will be;
> One went in front to point the Perfect Way,
> Who follows fears not where the end will be.[24]

A well-known hymn advises us, " 'Take up thy cross and follow me,' I heard my master say; 'I gave My life to ransom thee, Surrender your all today.' " Of course the hymn writer had biblical grounds for putting these words into Jesus' mouth. Matthew 16:24

says, "If anyone wants to come with me, he must forget himself, carry his cross, and follow me." Remember, the cross is rough and you might get splinters in your hands or ruin your manicure. You might even find that some will laugh at you for carrying your cross. But that is OK—they laughed at Jesus and he had the last laugh!

We are all on "free-agent" status until we sign on with someone. You could throw in with those who say the whole business of religion is for children or half-wits. You could align yourself with those who scoff at the credulity of "Jesus followers." Or you could sign on with those who have seen and experienced something significant in the life, the death, and the resurrection of the carpenter from Galilee. The going will be rough, and your journey sometimes shaky, but the destination is firm and the path secure.

# Notes

*Preface*

1. Thomas Albert Stafford, *Christian Symbolism in the Evangelical Churches* (New York: Abingdon-Cokesbury Press, 1952), p. 17.

2. Bruce Lockerbie, *The Timeless Moment* (Westchester, Il.: Cornerstone Books, 1980), p. 55.

3. Damasus Winzen, *Symbols of Christ* (New York: P. J. Kennedy and Sons, 1955), p. 13.

4. Frank Stagg, *Polarities of Man's Existence in Biblical Perspective* (Philadelphia: Westminster Press, 1973), p. 59.

*Chapter 1*

1. George Linnaeus Banks, "What I Live For," in *A Treasury of Inspiration*, edited by Ralph L. Woods (New York: Thomas Y. Crowell Co., 1951), pp. 409-410.

2. Andrew Gillies, "Two Prayers," in *The Treasury of Religious Verse*, Donald T. Kauffman, compiler (New York: Pillar Books, 1976 reprint), p. 161. Used by permission of the publisher.

*Chapter 2*

1. Martha Foote Crow, "The Wooden Christ," in *The Story of Jesus*, edited by Edward Wagenknecht (New York: Creative Age Press, 1946), p. 263.

2. Morris Bishop, "The Perforated Spirit," in *Professor in the Pulpit*, edited by W. Morgan Patterson and Raymond B. Brown (Nashville: Broadman Press, 1963), p. 20.

3. From *Light Armour* by Richard Armour. Copyright © 1979, McGraw-Hill Book Company. Used by permission.

4. Vic Oliver, as quoted by Laurence J. Peter, *Peter's Quotations* (New York: Bantam Books, 1979), p. 344.

5. Marilee Zdenek, quoted by Richard Anderson and Donald Deffner, *For Example* (St. Louis: Concordia Publishing House, 1977), p. 69.

6. George Buttrick, "Miracle on Main Street," in *The Meaning of These Things*, edited by Leonard Mann (Lima, Ohio: C.S.S. Publishing Company, 1977), p. 76.


*Chapter 3*

1. From *For Example*, written by Richard Anderson and Donald Deffner © 1977 Concordia Publishing House, pp. 204-205.

2. Robert Browning Hamilton, quoted in *Masterpieces of Religious Verse* © Copyright 1948 by Harper & Brothers, 1977 by Broadman Press.


*Chapter 4*

1. Milton Meyeroff, *On Caring* (New York: Harper & Row, "Perennial Library," n. d.), 54.

2. Ibid., p. 78.

3. Ibid., p. 80.


*Chapter 5*

1. Quoted in *The Choice Is Always Ours*, edited by Dorothy B. Phillips, Elizabeth B. Howes, and Lucille M. Nixon (New York: Pyramid Publications, 1975), p. 199.

2. Ibid., pp. 349-350.

3. Edgar A. Guest, "Failures," in *Treasury of Courage and Confidence*, edited by Norman Vincent Peale (Anderson, Ind.: Warner Press, 1974), p. 28.

4. Charles L. Wallis, editor, *Worship Resources for Special Days* (Grand Rapids: Baker Book House, 1976 reprint), p. 430.


*Chapter 6*

1. James F. White, *Introduction to Christian Worship* (Nashville: Abingdon Press, 1979), p. 235.

2. Dale Moody, *The Word of Truth* (Grand Rapids: William B. Eerdmans, 1980), pp. 471 ff.

3. Robert D. Young, *Be Brief About It* (Philadelphia: Westminster Press, 1980), p. 30.

4. Fisher Humphreys, *Thinking About God* (New Orleans: Insight Press, 1974), p. 196.

5. Samuel H. Miller, in *Preaching with Purpose and Power: Selected E. Y. Mullins Lectures*, edited by Don M. Aycock (Macon, Ga.: Mercer University Press, 1982), p. 241.

6. René Huyghe, quoted by Miller, *ibid.*

7. Walt Whitman, "When I Heard the Learn'd Astronomer," in *The Compact Treasury of Inspiration*, edited by Kenneth Soman Giniger (New York: Pocket Books, 1955), p. 166.

8. Eric C. Rust, "The Theology of the Lord's Supper," *Review & Expositor*, LXVI, (Winter, 1969), p. 37.

9. Rollo May, *Man's Search for Himself* (New York: W. W. Norton and Co., 1953), p. 14.

10. Lewis E. Rhodes, "The Sacrament of Wholeness," *Review & Expositor*, LXVI, (Winter, 1969), pp. 59-65.

11. William H. Willimon, *Worship As Pastoral Care* (Nashville: Abingdon Press, 1979), p. 174.

12. David Steele, "David Danced—Michal Wached," *Theology Today*, October, 1981, p. 359.

13. William E. Hulme, quoted by William Willimon, *Worship As Pastoral Care*, p. 177.

14. Frederick Buechner, *Wishful Thinking* (New York: Harper & Row, 1973), p. 53.

15. Ralph W. Sockman, *The Lord's Prayer* (New York: Abingdon-Cokesbury Press, 1947), the pages in this book are unnumbered.

*Chapter 7*

1. Alan W. Watts, quoted in *The Choice Is Always Ours*, edited by Dorothy Berkley Phillips, et al. (New York: Family Library, 1975, revised edition), pp. 96-97.

2. Wayne E. Oates, *Life's Detours* (Nashville: The Upper Room, 1974), p. 15.

3. Will D. Campbell, *Brother to a Dragonfly* (N.Y.: Seabury Press, 1977), pp. 219-220.

4. Orlo Strunk, Jr., *The Secret Self* (Nashville: Abingdon Press, 1976), pp. 81 ff.

5. Earl Koile, *Listening As a Way of Becoming* (Waco, Texas: Regency Books, 1977), p. 59.

6. Erich Lindemann, cited by Wayne E. Oates, *Pastoral Care and Counseling*

*in Grief and Separation* (Philadelphia: Fortress Press, 1976), p. 12, "Creative Pastoral Care and Counseling Series."

7. Huxley, quoted by Gerald Kennedy, *My Third Readers' Notebook* (Nashville: Abingdon Press, 1974), p. 183.

8. James D. Hamilton, *The Ministry of Pastoral Counseling* (Grand Rapids: Baker Book House, 1972), p. 15.

9. Reinhold Niebuhr, *Justice and Mercy*, edited by Ursula M. Niebuhr (New York: Harper and Row, 1974), flyleaf.

10. Wu Ming Fu, quoted in *The Choice Is Always Ours*, p. 42.

*Chapter 8*

1. The painting is reproduced in Roland H. Bainton's book, *Behold the Christ* (New York: Harper & Row, 1974), p. 96.

2. Ibid.

3. Albert McClellan, *The Hard Sayings of Jesus* (Nashville: Broadman Press, 1975), pp. 33-34.

4. Norman Nicholson, "The Ride to Jerusalem," in *The Story of Jesus in the World's Literature*, edited by Edward Wangenknecht. (New York: Creative Age Press, 1946), p. 284.

5. Quoted by Henry Sloane Coffin, *The Meaning of the Cross* (New York: Charles Scribner's Sons, 1931), pp. 52-53.

6. Quoted by Spencer Marsh, *God, Man, and Archie Bunker* (New York: Bantam Books, 1976), p. 44.

7. Quoted in *Notable Sermons from Protestant Pulpits*, edited by Charles R. Wallis (Nashville: Abingdon Press, 1958), p. 13.

8. William E. Hordern, *A Layman's Guide to Protestant Theology* (New York: Macmillan Publishing Co., 1968, revised edition), p. 198.

9. Ibid.

10. This painting can be seen in Cynthia Pearl Mauss's book, *Christ and the Fine Arts* (New York: Harper & Row, 1938), pp. 139-142.

11. This story is told by Sheldon B. Kopp, *If You Meet the Buddha on the Road, Kill Him!* (New York: Bantam Books, 1976), p. 106.

12. *Op. cit.*, p. 68.

13. Cited by Lawrence LeShan, *How to Meditate* (New York: Bantam Books, 1975), p. 33.

14. Henry Vaughn, "The Triumphant Entry," in *The Story of Jesus in the World's Literature*, pp. 284-285.

15. George Buttrick, *The Interpreter's Bible*, Vol. 7 (New York: Abingdon Press, 1951), p. 501.


*Chapter 9*

1. Harold A. Bosley, *The Deeds of Christ* (Nashville: Abingdon Press, 1969), p. 105.
2. This picture is found in Roland Bainton's book, *Behold the Christ* (New York: Harper & Row, 1974), p. 104.
3. Ibid., p. 105.
4. Richard Watson Gilder, "The Anger of Christ," in *The Story of Jesus in the World's Literature*, edited by Edward Wagenknecht (New York: Creative Age Press), pp. 287-288.
5. Ibid., p. 288.


*Chapter 10*

1. Frank Stagg, *New Testament Theology* (Nashville: Broadman Press, 1962), p. 135.
2. George Willard Benson, *The Cross: Its History and Symbolism* (New York: Hacker Art Books, 1976), pp. 14-15.
3. These examples are cited by Gerald O'Collins, *The Cross Today* (New York: Paulist Press, 1977), p. 41.
4. The information on the Venerable Bede is originally told by Gordon Huelin and is cited by O'Collins, *The Cross Today*, p. 41.
5. Ibid., p. 45.
6. Wayne E. Ward, *The Drama of Redemption* (Nashville: Broadman Press, 1966), pp. 108-109.
7. G. A. Studdert-Kennedy, "The Crucifixion," in *The Story of Jesus In The World's Literature*, edited by Edward Wagenknecht (New York: Creative Age Press, 1946), p. 348.
8. William F. Beck, *The New Testament in the Language of Today* (St. Louis: Concordia Publishing House, 1964).
9. George A. Buttrick, *Jesus Came Preaching* (Grand Rapids: Baker Book House, 1970 reprint), pp. 198-199.
10. Oscar F. Blackwelder, *The Interpreter's Bible* (New York: Abingdon Press, 1953), Vol. 10, p. 553.

11. Harold Cooke Phillips, in *Preaching with Purpose and Power,* edited by Don M. Aycock (Macon, Ga.: Mercer University Press, 1982), p. 304.

12. Harold E. Brierley, *What the Cross Means to Me* (London: James Clarke and Co.), p. 24.

13. Jurgen Möltmann, *The Crucified God,* translated by R. A. Wilson and John Bowden (New York: Harper and Row, 1974), p. 25.

14. Gerald O'Collins, *The Cross Today,* pp. 63-64.

15. W. L. Stidger, cited by Thomas A. Stafford, *Christian Symbolism* (New York: Abingdon Press, 1952), pp. 65-66.

16. Cited by Henry Sloane Coffin, *The Meaning of the Cross* (New York: Charles Scribner's Sons, 1931), p. 112.

17. Cited in *A Treasury of the Cross,* edited by Madeline S. Miller (New York: Harper and Brothers, 1956), p. 189.

18. George Willard Benson, *The Cross,* p. 190.

19. Harold Cooke Phillips, *Preaching with Purpose and Power,* p. 279.

20. Patrick White, cited by Gerald O'Collins, *The Cross Today,* unnumbered page across from the copyright page.

21. "For Me," anonymous in *Christ and the Fine Arts,* p. 406.

22. Charles McCoy and Marjorie Casebier McCoy, *The Transforming Cross* (Nashville: Abingdon Press, 1977), p. 105.

23. This analogy is told by Frank Stagg, *New Testament Theology,* pp. 147-148.

24. John Oxenham, "The Cross at the Crossway," in *A Treasury of the Cross,* p. 189.